P9-DJK-679

DEMCO

Fresh Ways
with Pastries & Sweets

Time-Life Books Inc.
is a wholly owned subsidiary of
TIME INCORPORATED

FOUNDER: Henry R. Luce 1898-1967

Editor-in-Chief: Jason McManus
Chairman and Chief Executive Officer: J. Richard Munro
President and Chief Operating Officer: N. J. Nicholas, Jr.
Editorial Director: Ray Cave
Executive Vice President, Books: Kelso F. Sutton
Vice President, Books: George Artandi

TIME-LIFE BOOKS INC.

EDITOR: George Constable
Executive Editor: Ellen Phillips
Director of Design: Louis Klein
Director of Editorial Resources: Phyllis K. Wise
Editorial Board: Russell B. Adams, Jr., Dale M. Brown,
Roberta Conlan, Thomas H. Flaherty, Lee Hassig, Donia
Ann Steele, Rosalind Stubenberg, Henry Woodhead
Director of Photography and Research: John
Conrad Weiser
Assistant Director of Editorial Resources: Elise
Ritter Gibson

EUROPEAN EDITOR: Kit van Tulleken
Assistant European Editor: Gillian Moore
Design Director: Ed Skyner
Chief of Research: Vanessa Kramer
Chief Sub-Editor: Ilse Gray

PRESIDENT: Christopher T. Linen
Chief Operating Officer: John M. Fahey, Jr.
Senior Vice Presidents: Robert M. DeSena, James L.
Mercer, Paul R. Stewart
Vice Presidents: Stephen L. Bair, Ralph J. Cuomo, Neal
Goff, Stephen L. Goldstein, Juanita T. James, Hallett
Johnson III, Carol Kaplan, Susan J. Maruyama, Robert
H. Smith, Joseph J. Ward
Director of Production Services: Robert J. Passantino

Library of Congress Cataloging in Publication Data
Fresh ways with pastries & sweets / by the editors of Time-Life
Books.
    p.   cm. — (Healthy home cooking)
  Includes index.
  ISBN 0-8094-6041-6.   ISBN 0-8094-6042-4 (lib. bdg.)
  1. Pastry.   2. Confectionery.
I. Time-Life Books.   II. Title: Fresh ways with pastries and
sweets.   III. Series.
TX773.F74 1988   641.8'65—dc19   88-20013

For information on and a full description of any Time-Life Books
series, please call 1-800-621-7026 or write:
Reader Information
Time-Life Customer Service
P.O. Box C-32068
Richmond, Virginia 23261-2068

Time-Life Books Inc. offers a wide range of fine recordings,
including a *Rock 'n' Roll Era* series. For subscription information,
call 1-800-621-7026 or write Time-Life Music, P.O. Box
C-32068, Richmond, Virginia 23261-2068.

HEALTHY HOME COOKING

SERIES DIRECTOR: Jackie Matthews
Studio Stylist: Liz Hodgson
Editorial Assistant: Eugénie Romer

Editorial Staff for *Fresh Ways with Pastries & Sweets:*
Editor: Frances Dixon
Researcher: Ellen Dupont
Designer: Paul Reeves
Sub-Editor: Christine Noble
Indexer: Myra Clark

PICTURE DEPARTMENT:
Administrator: Patricia Murray
Picture Coordinator: Amanda Hindley

EDITORIAL PRODUCTION:
Chief: Maureen Kelly
Assistant: Samantha Hill
Editorial Department: Theresa John, Debra Lelliott

U.S. Edition:
Assistant Editor: Barbara Fairchild Quarmby
Copy Coordinators: Marfé Ferguson Delano,
Colette Stockum
Picture Coordinator: Betty H. Weatherley

Editorial Operations
Copy Chief: Diane Ullius
Production: Celia Beattie
Library: Louise D. Forstall

Correspondents: Elizabeth Kraemer-Singh (Bonn);
Maria Vincenza Aloisi (Paris); Ann Natanson (Rome).

THE CONTRIBUTORS

JOANNA BLYTHMAN is a cook and recipe writer who
owns a specialty food shop in Edinburgh, Scotland. She
contributes articles on cooking to a number of newspa-
pers and periodicals.

LISA CHERKASKY has worked as a chef at numerous
restaurants in Washington, D.C., and in Madison, Wis-
consin, including nationally known Le Pavillon and Le Lion
d'Or. A graduate of The Culinary Institute of America at
Hyde Park, New York, she has also taught classes in French
cooking technique.

SILVIJA DAVIDSON studied at Leith's School of Food and
Wine in London and specializes in the development of
recipes from Latvia, as well as other international cuisines.

JANICE MURFITT trained as a home economist and has
worked as a food editor for *Family Circle* magazine. Her
books include *Cake Icing and Decorating* and *Cheesecakes and Flans.*

HILARY WALDEN is a food technologist and experienced
food writer. In addition to contributing to the major food
magazines, she has also written many books, including
Home Baking and *The Book of French Patisserie.*

The following people also have contributed recipes to this
volume: Maddalena Bonino, Joanna Farrow, Yvonne
Hamlett, Carole Handslip, Rosemary Wadey, Lorna Walk-
er, and Jeni Wright.

COVER
*Sugar-frosted rose and freesia petals decorate
miniature ring cakes filled with a kirsch-flavored
cream (recipe, page 70). A sparing amount of
cream, whipped to increase its bulk and
lightened with stiffly beaten egg white, provides a luxurious filling while keeping the calorie count low.*

THE COOKS

The recipes in this book were prepared for photographing
by Pat Alburey, Jacki Baxter, Jill Eggleton, Joanna Farrow,
Anne Gains, Carole Handslip, Dolly Meers, Janice Murfitt,
Jane Suthering, and Rosemary Wadey. *Studio Assistant:*
Rita Walters.

THE CONSULTANT

PAT ALBUREY is a home economist with a wide experi-
ence in preparing foods for photography, teaching cooking, and creating recipes. She has written a number of
cookbooks, including *The Harrods Book of Cakes and
Desserts,* and she was the studio consultant for the Time-
Life Books series The Good Cook. She has created a
number of the recipes in this volume.

THE NUTRITION CONSULTANT

PATRICIA JUDD trained as a dietician and worked in hos-
pital nutrition before returning to college to earn her
M.Sc. and Ph.D. degrees. She has since lectured in Nutrition and Dietetics at London University.

Nutritional analyses for *Fresh Ways with Pastries & Sweets*
were derived from McCance and Widdowson's *The Com-
position of Food* by A. A. Paul and D. A. T. Southgate, and
other current data.

Other Publications:

This volume is one of a series of illustrated cookbooks
that emphasize the preparation of healthful dishes for
today's weight-conscious, nutrition-minded eaters.

Fresh Ways with Pastries & Sweets

BY

THE EDITORS OF TIME-LIFE BOOKS

TIME-LIFE BOOKS / ALEXANDRIA, VIRGINIA

Contents

Quince and Chestnut Strudel

Honey and Hazelnut Tartlets

Caramel-Topped Apple Fingers

3 Delicate Confections.............102

Maple Sweetmeats

A Trio of Meringues

Spicy Pear Roulade

4 Pastry from the Microwave.............128

The New Pastry

As ravishing to the eye as it is delicious, pastry is the most bewitching branch of the culinary art. The simplest of ingredients—flour, sugar, butter, eggs, and cream—are transformed by the cook's alchemy into flaky shortcrust, tender chou-puff dough, melting meringue, and featherlight sponge cake, temptingly embellished with a choice of chocolates, nuts, fruit, and icing. The names of these confections are as beguiling as their appearance: Souffléed coffee diamonds (page 33), poppy-seed pillows (page 54), and chocolate kisses (page 107) are just some of the 120 recipes devised and selected for this volume.

Of course, no one eats such frivolities out of necessity; they are an indulgence, and so might seem to merit exclusion from a healthful diet. Fortunately, so harsh a regime is not necessary. By paring down the amounts of fat, cholesterol, and sugar, pastry can still be enjoyed in moderation. As a matter of fact, there is no reason why a 2,000-calorie daily diet should not include

both a pastry dessert and a sweet baked snack, provided fat and sugar levels in the rest of the day's meals are limited, for most of the recipes on the following pages contain fewer than 250 calories per portion.

Many of the featured recipes are new creations that satisfy the modern taste for lighter, more healthful food. Also included are versions of traditional French classics—meringue whirls, chocolate éclairs, iced petits fours, and other culinary gems that rank among the glories of the pastry cook's art. The special challenge of this volume has been to adapt these favorites to sensible dietary requirements, for traditionally it is the flavor and moistness of butter, the velvety smoothness of egg yolks, the richness of whipped cream, and the sweetness of sugar that contribute so much to their appeal.

Devising the new pastry

The challenge has been met in a combination of ways: by judiciously reducing the quantities of ingredients such as sugar and egg yolks, by replacing them with others that perform the same

purpose, and by using a light hand with fillings and final embellishments. These methods, devised and tested in the Healthy Home Cooking kitchens, produce delicious results with no sacrifice of flavor, texture, or appearance.

Sugar has been kept to a minimum by reducing, where possible, the quantity used in the basic doughs and batters, and by avoiding thick, sticky frostings and heavy, cloying fillings. Since sweetness is the essence of pastry, however, and sugar is an indispensable structural element of meringues and other confections, it is rarely omitted altogether.

Weight for weight, fats contribute about twice as many calories as sugar, so they too are included only in sufficient quantities to produce the desired result. Whereas most traditional recipes that use phyllo pastry call for a generous coating of butter between each layer, the recipes in this volume use only the merest film to achieve the same effect. Cream is used sparingly but seductively. When whipped cream is called for, the amount can be reduced by blending it with low-calorie beaten egg whites—as in the recipe for petal ring cakes on page 70. For some recipes, low-fat ricotta cheese or low-fat yogurt makes an excellent substitute for heavy cream.

When you use fat, the amount is not the only important consideration; the type of fat used is probably just as crucial. The choice lies between polyunsaturated fats, which are exclusively of vegetable origin, and saturated fats such as butter, which come mainly from animal sources. Saturated fats raise the level of blood cholesterol, and a high level of blood cholesterol is implicated in heart disease. Polyunsaturated fats do not raise the level of blood cholesterol and may actually lower it.

In practical terms, the choice is between soft polyunsaturated margarine and butter; many hard margarines contain almost as much saturated fat as butter, whereas oils of whatever type will not incorporate air when beaten and thus have a limited application in pastry making. Equal quantities of fat, incidentally, contain more or less an equal number of calories.

Dietary considerations alone would dictate the use of polyunsaturated margarine. Taste, however, counsels the use of butter, which has an incomparable flavor. Common sense suggests a compromise. In this volume, butter is only specified when its unique qualities make a distinct difference to the final product. All the other recipes recommend the use of polyunsaturated margarine. Obviously, these instructions may be tailored to suit individual needs and preferences.

Certain foods contain cholesterol itself, which can contribute to raising blood-cholesterol levels. Egg yolks, an indispensable ingredient of many pastry creations, contain large amounts of cholesterol. Although dietary cholesterol is not so important a contributor to blood cholesterol as the type we make ourselves from saturated fat, it is nonetheless good dietary practice to eat cholesterol-rich foodstuffs in moderation. In some preparations, egg yolks traditionally serve as the main binding agent, but substitutions can be devised.

The new thinking is demonstrated in the four standard recipes presented on pages 10 and 11. Many pastries are assemblies of precooked ingredients, and these four key recipes provide the bases for the confections that appear later as well as for your own creations. Sponge cake is usually made with a ratio of 4 eggs to 4 ounces of flour, but one of the egg yolks is omitted on page 11, and an egg white is added to help bind the mixture and make it rise. The amount of butter is also less than that usually specified.

Pastry cream, another standby of classic French pastries, is a custard thickened primarily with egg yolks, but the recipe on page 11 replaces some of the egg yolks with cornstarch and egg white. The chou-puff dough on page 10 is made with half the eggs usually required and half the butter. The shortcrust dough on the same page is not enriched with eggs and sugar, as in many classic pastry recipes, and it calls for polyunsaturated margarine. In short, all the cornerstones of classic pastry making have been re-created in a more healthful mold.

The right ingredients used correctly

The lightest sponge cakes, the crispest tartlet cases, the airiest meringues, and the most tender chou-puff dough require the most refined ingredients if they are to achieve the sweet and fleeting perfection that is the hallmark of good pastry. For this reason, sifted white flour is generally used in preference to whole-wheat flour, which produces heavier, denser baked goods with a pronounced nutty flavor. White sugar is the main sweetening agent for most pastries. Brown sugars, which are not nutritionally superior to the more refined variety, are sometimes chosen for their more assertive flavor, or to impart a golden color to a meringue or pastry base. Honey has an advantage over commercial sugars in that—weight for weight—it possesses one and a half times the sweetening power. It is included in the apple

and pear upside-down tartlets on page 17 and the honey and hazelnut tartlets on page 29, but its distinctive flavor rules it out as an all-purpose sweetening agent.

Egg whites play a vital role in imparting lightness to cakes, mousses, and fillings without adding fat or cholesterol and at a minimal caloric cost; there are fewer than 20 calories in an egg white. To prepare egg whites for beating, they must be carefully separated from the yolks, which contain fat that prevents the whites from rising properly. Eggs can be separated either by letting the white drip between the fingers into a bowl or by passing the yolk between the halves of the egg shell so that the white falls into the bowl. In either case, if the recipe calls for a number of egg whites, it is wise to drop each white in turn into a small bowl before adding it to the rest; in this way, if a yolk should break and mix with the white, it will not spoil the other whites. Beaters and bowls must be scrupulously clean, and plastic should never be used since it harbors traces of fat. Bowls made of glass, china, or—best of all—copper are recommended.

The delicate mousses used as fillings and toppings in this volume are made with low-fat yogurt lightened with egg whites and stiffened with gelatin. These mousses have fewer calories than the egg and cream enriched versions used in traditional pastries. Powdered gelatin is preferable to leaf gelatin because it is easier to obtain and to measure.

Fruit is given a prominent place in many of the recipes because of its intrinsic sweetness, vibrant colors, and delicious flavors. It is healthful, too—high in fiber, vitamins, and minerals and low in calories. Like honey, fruit owes its natural sweetness to the presence of fructose. Choose fresh, ripe fruit. Canned fruit should be avoided since neither its flavor nor appearance can match that of fresh fruit, but frozen fruit provides an adequate substitute when fresh varieties are out of season. Frozen raspberries, blackberries, cranberries, gooseberries, and rhubarb work well in sauces and purées. In many produce shops and supermarkets, imported tropical fruit is as familiar as domestic varieties; the general availability of such formerly exotic items as kumquats, passionfruit, New Zealand gooseberries, and kiwi fruit is reflected in the recipes.

Finishing touches

At the tables of the European nobility during the 18th and 19th centuries, pastries were so heavily and fancifully decorated that one of the greatest pastry cooks of the period, Antonin Carême, likened them to architecture rather than cookery. Happily for the home cook, such excessive ornamentation is no longer considered either necessary or desirable for the creation of beautiful pastries. The decorations shown on the following pages are both elegant in their simplicity and well within the reach of most

The Key to Better Eating

Healthy Home Cooking addresses the concerns of today's weight-conscious, health-minded cooks with recipes that take into account guidelines set by nutritionists. The secret to eating well, of course, has to do with maintaining a balance of foods in the diet. The recipes should therefore be used thoughtfully, in the context of a day's eating. To make the choice easier, this book offers an analysis of the nutrients in each recipe, as in the sample at right. The analysis is for a single cake or pastry, or an individual serving of a larger item. The counts that are given for calories, protein, cholesterol, total fat, saturated fat, and sodium are approximate.

Interpreting the chart

The chart at right shows the National Research Council's Recommended Dietary Allowances of calories and protein for healthy men, women, and children, along with the council's recommendations for the "safe and adequate" intake of sodium. Although the council has not established recommendations for either cholesterol or fat, the chart includes what the National Institutes of Health and the American Heart Association consider the daily maximum amounts for healthy members of the population. The Heart Association, among other groups, has pointed out that Americans derive about 40 percent of their calories from fat; this, it believes, should be cut to less than 30 percent.

The volumes in the Healthy Home Cooking series do not purport to be diet books, nor do they focus on health foods. Rather, they express a commonsense approach to cooking that uses salt, sugar, cream, butter, and oil in moderation while employing other ingredients that also provide flavor and satisfaction. In these pastry recipes, nuts, spices, fruit, peels, juices, and wines and liqueurs are all used toward this end.

In this volume, a conscious effort has been made to limit the cakes, pastries, and sweets to 250 calories per serving, and to restrict the

Calories **250**
Protein **23g.**
Cholesterol **70mg.**
Total fat **11g.**
Saturated fat **3g.**
Sodium **185mg.**

amount of total fat and saturated fat to 10 and 5 grams, respectively, per helping. Occasionally, in the interest of taste, texture, or even the successful cooking of a pastry, the amount of sugar or fat has been increased. When a recipe exceeds the 250-calorie limit, the cook should cut back a little elsewhere in the daily menu.

The recipes make few unusual demands. Naturally, they call for fresh ingredients, offering substitutes when these are unavailable. (Only the original ingredient is calculated in the nutrient analysis, however.) Most of the ingredients can be found in any well-stocked supermarket. Any that may seem unfamiliar are described in a glossary on pages 138 and 139. In order to help the cook

master new techniques, how-to photographs appear wherever appropriate.

About cooking times

Because the recipes emphasize fresh foods, they may take a bit longer to prepare than dishes that call for packaged products, but the payoff in flavor, and often in nutrition, should compensate for the little extra time involved. To help the cook plan ahead, Healthy Home Cooking provides "working" and "total" times for each recipe.

Working time denotes the minutes actively spent on preparation; since no two cooks work at exactly the same speed, it is, of course, approximate. Total time includes any soaking or chilling specified in the recipe, and it includes unattended cooking time; again, because of the variations in ovens and cake and tartlet molds, the cooking times given can only be an average. Total time also includes the minutes—or even hours—that the finished product takes to cool to room temperature or set completely. (Cooling and setting times can vary according to the temperature and humidity of the kitchen.)

Recommended Dietary Guidelines

		Average Daily Intake		Maximum Daily Intake			
		CALORIES	PROTEIN grams	CHOLESTEROL milligrams	TOTAL FAT grams	SATURATED FAT grams	SODIUM milligrams
Children	7-10	2400	22	240	80	27	1800
Females	11-14	2200	37	220	73	24	2700
	15-18	2100	44	210	70	23	2700
	19-22	2100	44	300	70	23	3300
	23-50	2000	44	300	67	22	3300
	51-75	1800	44	300	60	20	3300
Males	11-14	2700	36	270	90	30	2700
	15-18	2800	56	280	93	31	2700
	19-22	2900	56	300	97	32	3300
	23-50	2700	56	300	90	30	3300
	51-75	2400	56	300	80	27	3300

cooks, providing a final flourish that does not require hours of labor in the kitchen or add scores of unwanted calories to the finished product.

A dusting of confectioners' sugar is sufficient embellishment for most small cakes and pastries. Various patterns can be made by masking part of the cake with pieces of cardboard before sprinkling the sugar. A similar effect but in a different color may be achieved by using cocoa powder. Confectioners' sugar can be dissolved in water or fruit juice to make a thin icing for spooning or piping over a cake or pastry. Instead of applying a uniform coating, pipe a few threads on the pastry to create maximum visual effect with minimum calories.

The glossy sheen of a caramel coating enhances the appearance of both pastries and sweets, and the crisp, sweet texture is well worth the effort that making caramel entails. It is prepared by heating sugar with water until the sugar becomes pale brown and fragrant. The cooking process is arrested by dipping the pan in cold water; then the pan is placed in a bowl of hot water to keep the caramel fluid during the time it takes to apply it. It is important to disturb the caramel as little as possible to prevent it from forming crystals, which spoil its texture.

Jam, in all its bright colors and sweet flavors, provides an attractive finishing touch. The red-currant jelly coating on the strawberry tartlets on page 19 intensifies the color of the fruit and makes it even more jewel-like; apricot jam spread on an apple tart produces a golden glaze that also helps bring out the flavor of the fruit (page 16); raspberry jam piped in a flower pattern makes a delicate embellishment to petits fours (page 106).

Of all the elements used in pastry making, chocolate is the ingredient that for many people most symbolizes luxurious self-indulgence. The richness and smoothness of chocolate is achieved during manufacture by adding extra cocoa butter to the ground beans, which are sweetened by the addition of large quantities of sugar—up to 60 percent of the final weight—and sometimes given a milder flavor by the addition of milk. Because of the presence of fats, even semisweet chocolate has a caloric content about one and a half times that of sugar; milk chocolate, with only about 1 percent more fat, is not significantly higher in calories. The health-conscious cook should buy the best-quality dark chocolate available, which will contain at least 52 percent cocoa solids and correspondingly less sugar. The stronger flavor of such chocolate means that a little goes a long way.

Even used sparingly, chocolate produces striking decorative effects thanks to its unique consistency. Chocolate melted over low heat liquefies, and in this form can be piped or drizzled into patterns, used for dipping small cakes and sweets, or poured into a flat tray where it sets into a thin sheet as it cools. Once set, the chocolate can be cut into squares to make boxes for petits fours (page 132) or shaved paper thin with a sharp knife to make scrolls. These techniques are explained on pages 12 and 13.

Necessary equipment

A kitchen fully equipped for making pastries may contain a bewildering variety of pans, pastry cutters, piping tips, and molds of all shapes and sizes, special tools for pitting cherries and for scraping ribbons of zest from citrus fruit, in addition to a powerful hand beater and a sturdy food processor. Many of these items, though useful and labor saving, are not absolutely necessary. Food processors and electric beaters certainly save time, but their work can usually be done with the aid of sharp knives, a wooden spoon, or a wire whisk, as the case may be. So long as the dimensions of the pan you substitute are the same, tartlets can be made in standard muffin pans instead of in the range of exotically shaped pans suggested by the recipes. Cherries can be pitted with a small, sharp knife, and citrus zest can be removed with a vegetable peeler and then cut into shreds.

The truly indispensable implements for making pastry are accurate kitchen scales and a set of measuring spoons; exact quantities are important to the success of cakes and pastries. While a sugar thermometer is not necessary for some recipes, such as caramel, which is easy to judge by eye as the sugar darkens, other stages of sugar syrup, such as soft crack (page 127), are most accurately gauged with a candy thermometer to ensure that they are neither too sticky nor too brittle.

A good working knowledge of your oven is also essential, for cooking times can vary widely from oven to oven. Cooking times and temperatures given in the recipes are for conventional ovens; if you have a convection oven, which circulates heat more quickly, keep to the recommended cooking time and lower the temperature by up to 75° F. Use the manufacturer's guidelines. Microwave ovens are not only invaluable for preparing some ingredients—such as firm fruit that needs cooking—for final assembly, but they may also produce finished pastries in their own right. The recipes on pages 129 to 137 illustrate the versatility of these time-saving machines.

Pastries may be enjoyed with any meal, but perhaps they are best appreciated on their own, served with tea, coffee, or a fruit drink to make a soothing interlude at midmorning or in the afternoon. By exercising complete control over the ingredients used in homemade pastries, you can enjoy such welcome moments without departing from a healthful diet.

Four Essential Recipes

Shortcrust Dough

Makes about 9 ounces
Working (and total) time: about 10 minutes

1½ cups unbleached all-purpose flour
1 tsp. sugar
6 tbsp. polyunsaturated margarine, chilled
1 egg white, lightly beaten

Sift the flour and sugar into a mixing bowl. Add the margarine, and rub it into the dry ingredients with your fingertips until the mixture resembles fine bread-crumbs. Add the egg white, mixing it in with a wooden spoon to form a dough. Gather the dough into a firm ball, and knead it briefly on a lightly floured surface until it is smooth; do not overwork the dough, or it will become oily and the baked pastry will be tough. Roll out the dough as required.

EDITOR'S NOTE: *Shortcrust dough may be stored, tightly covered with plastic wrap, in the refrigerator for up to a week, or in the freezer for up to three months.*

Chou-Puff Dough

Working (and total) time: about 15 minutes

1 cup unbleached all-purpose flour
⅛ tsp. salt
5 tbsp. unsalted butter
2 eggs
1 egg white

Sift the flour and salt onto a sheet of wax paper. Put the butter and 1 cup of water into a heavy-bottomed pan, and heat on low until the butter melts. Increase the heat to medium high and bring to a boil. Remove the pan from the heat and slide in all the flour, beating vigorously with a wooden spoon. Return the pan to the heat and continue beating the mixture until it forms a ball. Allow the mixture to cool for a few minutes.

Lightly beat the eggs and egg white together. Using an electric hand-held mixer, or beating vigorously with a wooden spoon, gradually incorporate the eggs into the cooled mixture. Beat well after each addition and continue until the mixture forms a smooth shiny paste.

EDITOR'S NOTE: *Uncooked chou-puff dough does not keep; it should be used immediately. Once cooked, however, chou puffs may be frozen, then thawed and filled at a later date. The recipes in Chapter 1 calling for chou-puff dough either use the full quantity made here, or, if less is required, list the necessary ingredients within the individual ingredients lists.*

Sponge Cake

Makes one 12-by-8-inch cake
Working time: about 20 minutes
Total time: about 1 hour

3 eggs
1 egg white
½ cup sugar
1 cup unbleached all-purpose flour
2 tbsp. unsalted butter, melted and slightly cooled

Preheat the oven to 350° F. Butter a 12-by-8-by-1½-inch rectangular cake pan, and line the bottom with parchment paper.

Put the eggs, egg white, and sugar into a mixing bowl. Set the bowl over a saucepan of hot but not boiling water on low heat. Using an electric hand-held mixer, beat the eggs and sugar together until the mixture is thick and very pale. Remove the bowl from the saucepan, and continue beating until the mixture is cool and falls from the beater in a ribbon. Sift the flour very lightly over the surface of the egg and sugar mixture, then fold it in gently using a large rubber spatula. Gradually fold in the melted butter.

Pour the sponge batter into the prepared pan and spread it evenly. Bake until it is well risen, springy to the touch, and very slightly shrunk from the sides of the pan—25 to 30 minutes. Carefully unmold the cake onto a wire rack. Loosen the parchment paper but do not remove it. Place another wire rack on top of the paper, then invert both racks together so that the cake is right side up on top of the paper. Remove the top rack and allow the cake to cool.

EDITOR'S NOTE: *Individual recipes do not always use the full quantity of sponge cake prepared here. Leftover cake may be stored in an airtight container for several days and used on another occasion; several of the recipes in Chapter 3 make use of sponge-cake trimmings.*

Pastry Cream

Makes about 1¼ cups
Working time: about 25 minutes
Total time: about 1 hour and 50 minutes
(includes chilling)

2 egg yolks
2½ tbsp. sugar
¼ cup unbleached all-purpose flour
1½ tbsp. cornstarch, sifted
1¼ cups skim milk
1 tsp. pure vanilla extract
2 tbsp. sour cream
1 egg white

Put the egg yolks and half the sugar into a bowl. Beat them together until the mixture is thick, then carefully fold in the flour and cornstarch.

Heat the milk and vanilla extract together in a saucepan until the liquid is hot but not boiling. Gradually beat the hot milk into the egg mixture, then strain the mixture, through a fine sieve, back into the pan. Stir the custard over low heat until it comes to a boil, then simmer it, stirring continuously, for five to six minutes; do not let the custard burn during this time. Remove the pan from the heat, spoon the custard into a bowl, and cover the surface closely with plastic wrap to prevent a skin from forming. Set the custard aside for about 10 minutes, then refrigerate until it is cool but not cold—15 to 20 minutes.

Whip the custard until it is smooth, then beat in the sour cream. In another bowl, beat the egg white until it is stiff, then whip in the remaining sugar until the mixture is shiny. Gradually fold the egg white into the custard. Cover the bowl with plastic wrap and refrigerate the pastry cream for at least one hour.

Orange-flavored pastry cream. Add the finely grated zest of 1 orange to the milk. Whip 1 tablespoon of orange-flavored liqueur into the cooled custard before adding the beaten egg white.

Chocolate-flavored pastry cream. Melt 1 ounce of semisweet chocolate in the hot milk in the saucepan.

Liqueur-flavored pastry cream. Whip 1 tablespoon of brandy, rum, kirsch, or a coffee- or almond-flavored liqueur into the cooled custard before adding the beaten egg white.

EDITOR'S NOTE: *The pastry cream may be stored in the refrigerator for up to two days.*

Making the Most of Chocolate

For the health-conscious pastry cook, chocolate poses a challenge. Greatly desirable for its incomparable flavor and luxurious smoothness, it is undeniably high in fat and calories: 1 ounce of semisweet chocolate contains 143 calories and 10 grams of fat, of which 6 grams are saturated fat. The creative answer to this dilemma is to make a little chocolate go a long way.

In place of a thick chocolate icing, a sprinkling of grated chocolate provides an appetizing finish for pastries. For decoration, you can also shave chocolate into scrolls *(right)*, cut a thin sheet into geometric shapes *(below)*, or pipe it into edible embroidery *(opposite)* using a parchment-paper or wax-paper pastry bag.

Chocolate easily scorches if exposed to direct heat. To melt chocolate, break it into pieces and place it in a flameproof bowl. Fill a saucepan one-quarter full of water and bring it to a simmer. Set the bowl over the pan. Stir the chocolate with a wooden spoon until it is smooth.

Miniature Scrolls

1 *SPREADING THE CHOCOLATE. Brush a work surface with oil to prevent sticking. Melt chocolate in a bowl set over a saucepan of hot water, then pour the chocolate onto the work surface. Using a flexible metal spatula, spread the chocolate in as thin a layer as possible; let it cool and set.*

2 *FORMING THE SCROLLS. Push the edge of a knife blade or a stiff, wide-bladed scraper into the chocolate at a low angle. Use a continuous motion to roll the chocolate into miniature scrolls.*

Smooth Squares and Rectangles

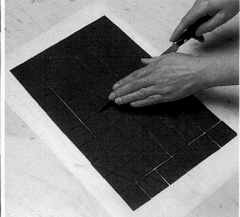

1 *SMOOTHING THE CHOCOLATE. Grease a jelly-roll pan, and line it with wax paper or parchment paper. Melt chocolate in a bowl set over hot water and pour it into the pan to form a layer ¹⁄₁₀ inch deep. Rap the pan on the work surface to eliminate air bubbles, then smooth the chocolate with a flexible metal spatula.*

2 *UNMOLDING THE SHEET. Allow the chocolate to harden in a cool place for about 30 minutes. Place a sheet of wax paper or parchment paper on the surface; invert the pan. Lift the pan and peel away the lining paper.*

3 *CUTTING THE SHAPES. Using a long, sharp knife or cutters, cut the chocolate sheet into the desired shapes—here 1½-inch squares. For squares or rectangles, use a ruler to measure the intervals, and nick the edges of the chocolate sheet with the tip of a small, sharp knife.*

Delicate Tracery

1 *CUTTING A TRIANGLE. Cut out a 12-inch square of wax paper or parchment paper. Fold the square in half diagonally, then cut along the crease. Reserve one triangle.*

2 *FOLDING THE TRIANGLE. Place the triangle on the work surface with its right angle at the bottom right-hand corner. Place the fingers of your left hand on the middle of the edge nearest you and grasp the left-hand corner with your right hand; pull it over your left hand to meet the right-angled corner.*

3 *MAKING A CONE. Tuck the two corners under the fingers of your left hand. With your right hand, grasp the corner farthest from you and wrap it around your left hand to make a cone with a fine point. Fold the three corners down together. Fill the paper cone two-thirds full with melted chocolate.*

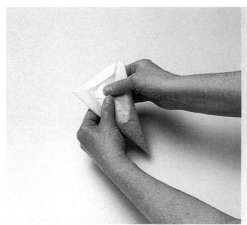

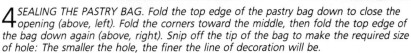

4 *SEALING THE PASTRY BAG. Fold the top edge of the pastry bag down to close the opening (above, left). Fold the corners toward the middle, then fold the top edge of the bag down again (above, right). Snip off the tip of the bag to make the required size of hole: The smaller the hole, the finer the line of decoration will be.*

5 *PIPING THE CHOCOLATE. Hold the pastry bag between your fingers and thumb, at an angle of 45 degrees to the surface and just above it. Squeeze gently and pipe toward yourself, raising the bag slightly as the chocolate falls onto the surface. For a zigzag effect, move the bag from side to side. To finish, lower the tip and pull the bag away sharply.*

1 *Crisp pastry cases stand ready to be filled with a selection of colorful fresh fruit (recipe, page 20).*

Happy Unions of Pastry and Filling

The creations of the pastry chef—and the art of classic French patisserie—are based on the pastry itself, which is the perfect foil for velvety creams and custards, chocolate and caramel, fruit and nuts. Flaky pastries depend for their success on such a high butter content that they have no place in a volume on healthful cooking. But shortcrust, chou-puff, and phyllo pastries make such adaptable foundations that the omissions will cause no hardship.

Shortcrust, the basis of crisp tartlet shells, is simplicity itself to make, requiring only cool ingredients mixed with a light hand for perfect results. Polyunsaturated margarine, which remains soft even at fairly low temperatures, must be thoroughly chilled. Rub it gently into the flour with the fingertips only, lifting and sifting the flour at the same time. As soon as the mixture looks like breadcrumbs, stop rubbing or it will become oily. Egg white rather than water is used to bind the dry ingredients, which reduces shrinkage when the dough is baked. The dough should be rolled no more than is necessary; shortcrust pastry that is overworked becomes tough.

Patient preparation is the only requisite for chou-puff dough, the starting point for the tender éclairs, puffs, and fingers on pages 34 to 47. Add the eggs a little at a time, beating vigorously between each addition to incorporate as much air as possible. Your reward comes when the dough is baked, rising to four times its original volume, or even more if steam is trapped in the baking process as in the recipe for peach puffs on page 36.

Once baked, chou pastry cases can be kept in a cool place, covered with foil, for up to eight hours before they are filled. They will soften quickly when filled, so prepare them for the table no more than one or two hours before serving, or as the recipe directs.

Phyllo, a traditional Middle Eastern pastry, has a low fat content and a subtle flavor, making it the perfect partner for richly spiced fruit-and-nut mixtures. Used paper thin and built up in layers, it can be formed into any number of shapes—from simple rolled strudel *(page 52)* to fans *(page 48)*, cigars *(page 58)*, and petal cases filled with fruit *(page 59)*.

Apple Slice

THIS IS A VARIATION ON THE TRADITIONAL FRENCH
APPLE TART: HERE, THE DELICATE FLAVOR OF LIME ADDS
SUBTLETY TO THE APPLE FILLING.

Serves 8
Working time: about 45 minutes
Total time: about 2 hours and 20 minutes

Calories **260**
Protein **3g.**
Cholesterol **0mg.**
Total fat **11g.**
Saturated fat **2g.**
Sodium **100mg.**

1¼ cups whole-wheat flour
1 tsp. light brown sugar
6 tbsp. polyunsaturated margarine, chilled
1 oz. hazelnuts, toasted, peeled (technique, page 29), and ground (about ¼ cup)
1 egg white
1 tbsp. apricot jam without added sugar
Apple-lime filling
2 lb. cooking apples, peeled, cored, and sliced
1 lime, grated zest and juice
7 tbsp. sugar
2 sweet apples
2 tsp. confectioners' sugar

Lightly butter a 14-by-4½-inch rectangular fluted or plain tart pan with a removable bottom, and place it on a baking sheet.

To make the dough, sift the flour and sugar into a mixing bowl. Rub in the margarine with your fingertips until the mixture resembles fine breadcrumbs, then blend in the ground hazelnuts and the egg white with

a wooden spoon to form a dough. Knead the dough briefly on a lightly floured surface until it is smooth, then roll it out into a rectangle 1 inch larger all around than the pan. Lift the dough with the rolling pin, and ease it into the bottom and up the sides of the pan, pressing it into the fluted edges. Trim off excess dough with a knife and prick the inside with a fork. Chill the dough while preparing the filling.

Preheat the oven to 375° F.

Place the cooking apples in a large, nonreactive saucepan with the grated lime zest, half the juice, and 2 tablespoons of water. Cover, bring to a boil, then cook over low heat, stirring occasionally, until the apples are tender and pulpy. Stir in the sugar and boil off any excess juice, then remove the saucepan from the heat and allow the mixture to cool. Peel, core, and thinly slice the sweet apples. Toss the slices in the remaining lime juice to prevent discoloration.

Spread the cooked apple mixture in the pastry shell and arrange overlapping apple slices on top. Sift the confectioners' sugar over the apple slices. Place the tart pan on a baking sheet, and bake the tart until the pastry is golden brown and the apple slices have browned at the edges—30 to 40 minutes.

In a small pan set over low heat, warm the apricot jam with a tablespoon of water until it becomes liquid. Press the liquid jam through a fine sieve, then use a pastry brush to spread the glaze over the apple slices.

Allow the tart to cool fully in the pan, then carefully unmold it and cut it into slices for serving.

Apple and Pear Upside-Down Tartlets

BECAUSE THE TARTLETS ARE BAKED UPSIDE DOWN, THE PASTRY REMAINS CRISP AS THE FRUIT BELOW IS COOKED BY THE HEAT OF THE OVEN CONDUCTED THROUGH THE PAN.

Makes 6 tartlets
Working time: about 35 minutes
Total time: about 1 hour and 10 minutes

Per tartlet:
Calories **210**
Protein **3g.**
Cholesterol **0mg.**
Total fat **8g.**
Saturated fat **2g.**
Sodium **100mg.**

6 oz. shortcrust dough (recipe, page 10) made with ¾ tsp. ground cinnamon added to the dry ingredients
2 tbsp. honey
3 small sweet apples
3 small firm pears
2 tsp. fresh lemon juice

Cover the dough tightly with plastic wrap and chill it while making the filling.

Preheat the oven to 400° F. Lightly butter six 4-inch fluted tartlet pans. Boil the honey in a small saucepan for one minute. Pour a little hot honey into the buttered pans, evenly coating their bottoms. Peel, core, and thinly slice the apples and pears, and toss the slices in the lemon juice to prevent discoloration. Arrange alternate layers of apples and pears in each pan, overlapping the slices in each layer. (Arrange the bottom layer of slices particularly carefully; this will be the top when the tartlets are inverted.) The layered fruit should rise slightly above the top of the pan.

Cut the dough into six equal pieces, and roll out each piece on a lightly floured surface into a circle a little wider than the top of a pan. Neaten the edges, then place the pastry circles over the fruit, tucking their edges inside the pans. Seal the pastry to the fluted rims of the pans by pressing with your fingers all around the inside edges.

Bake the tartlets until the pastry is golden brown— 25 to 30 minutes. Leave them in their pans for a few minutes, then invert them onto serving plates. Serve the tartlets warm or cold.

EDITOR'S NOTE: *If you like, a little extra honey can be drizzled over the top of the tartlets for serving.*

Jam Tartlets

Makes 18 tartlets
Working time: about 25 minutes
Total time: about 1 hour and 10 minutes

Per tartlet:
Calories **95**
Protein **1g.**
Cholesterol **0mg.**
Total fat **4g.**
Saturated fat **1g.**
Sodium **45mg.**

9 oz. shortcrust dough (recipe, page 10)
⅓ cup red jam (strawberry, raspberry, or black currant) without added sugar
1 candied pear, thinly sliced (optional)
⅓ cup apricot jam without added sugar
1 candied fig, thinly sliced (optional)

Preheat the oven to 425° F.

On a lightly floured surface, roll out the dough to a thickness of about ⅛ inch. Cut out 18 circles with a 3-inch pastry cutter, reserving the trimmings. Ease the circles into 2½-inch tartlet pans, prick the inside sur- faces all over with the tines of a fork, then chill the tartlet cases for 30 minutes.

Roll out the reserved pastry trimmings, and cut them into petal or diamond shapes with a sharp knife. Put the shapes on a baking sheet and bake them together with the chilled tartlet cases. Remove the cases from the oven after seven minutes; continue baking the pastry shapes until they are golden brown—two to three minutes more.

Spoon 2 rounded teaspoons of red jam into half the tartlet cases and decorate with slices of candied pear, if you are using it. Fill the remaining tartlet cases with the apricot jam and top with the fig slices if you wish. Return the tartlets to the oven, and bake them until the pastry is golden brown and the jam is bubbling—five to seven minutes.

Unmold the tartlets onto a wire rack to cool. Before serving, decorate them with the pastry shapes.

Strawberry Tartlets

Makes 18 tartlets
Working time: about 25 minutes
Total time: about 1 hour and 10 minutes

Per tartlet:
Calories **95**
Protein **1g.**
Cholesterol **0mg.**
Total fat **4g.**
Saturated fat **1g.**
Sodium **45mg.**

9 oz. shortcrust dough (recipe, page 10)	
10 oz. strawberries, hulled and halved	
6 tbsp. red-currant jelly	
1½ tbsp. anise-flavored liqueur	

Preheat the oven to 425° F.

On a lightly floured surface, roll out the dough to a thickness of about ⅛ inch. Using a 3-inch cutter, cut 18 circles and use these to line 2½-inch tartlet pans. Prick the inside surfaces with a fork, then chill the cases for 30 minutes.

Bake the tartlet cases until they are golden brown—15 to 20 minutes. Remove them from the oven, allow them to cool a little, then unmold them onto a wire rack set over a tray.

Arrange the halved strawberries in the tartlet cases. To prepare the glaze, place the red-currant jelly in a small, nonreactive pan with 1½ tablespoons of water. Stir over low heat until the jelly has melted, then stir in the liqueur. Using a pastry brush, spread a generous amount of warm glaze over each tartlet; reheat the glaze if it begins to set.

Fresh Fruit Tartlets with Passionfruit Cream

Makes 12 tartlets
Working time: about 45 minutes
Total time: about 1 hour and 15 minutes

Per tartlet:
Calories **140**
Protein **3g.**
Cholesterol **trace**
Total fat **7g.**
Saturated fat **2g.**
Sodium **75mg.**

9 oz. shortcrust dough (recipe, page 10)
½ mango
½ kiwi fruit
12 small strawberries
2 kumquats
12 seedless green grapes
½ pomegranate
1 passionfruit
Passionfruit cream
1 passionfruit, or 2 tbsp. fresh orange juice
6 tbsp. sour cream
1 tsp. sugar

Preheat the oven to 425° F. On a lightly floured surface, roll out the dough to a thickness of about ⅛ inch. Cut out 12 circles with a 4-inch pastry cutter, and ease them into 3-inch shallow tartlet pans. Prick the inside surfaces with a fork and chill the cases for 30 minutes.

Bake the chilled tartlet cases until they are light brown—15 to 20 minutes. Allow them to cool a little before unmolding them onto a wire rack.

While the tartlet cases are baking, prepare the fruit. Peel and thinly slice the mango and kiwi fruit; hull and halve the strawberries; thinly slice the kumquats and discard the seeds; halve the grapes; remove the pomegranate seeds; cut the passionfruit in half widthwise, and spoon out the pulp and seeds.

To prepare the passionfruit cream, cut the fruit in half, spoon out the pulp and seeds, and blend them into the sour cream. Alternatively, blend the orange juice and sour cream together. Add the sugar and beat until the mixture is smooth. Spoon the fruit cream into the pastry shells.

Decorate the tartlets with the prepared fresh fruit, filling any gaps with the passionfruit.

EDITOR'S NOTE: *If you are not serving the tartlets immediately, brush the fruit with an apricot glaze: In a small, nonreactive pan, heat 2 tablespoons of apricot jam without added sugar and 2 tablespoons of water, then press the liquid jam through a fine-mesh sieve. Serve the tartlets within 24 hours of their preparation.*

Green Grape Tartlets

Makes 12 tartlets
Working time: about 35 minutes
Total time: about 2 hours (includes chilling)

Per tartlet:
Calories **140**
Protein **3g.**
Cholesterol **trace**
Total fat **6g.**
Saturated fat **2g.**
Sodium **70mg.**

9 oz. shortcrust dough (recipe, page 10)
24 large firm seedless green grapes
4 tbsp. sour cream
Wine syrup
½ cup sweet white dessert wine
1 tbsp. sugar
½ orange, zest only, cut into several pieces
1½ tsp. powdered gelatin

Preheat the oven to 425° F. Roll out the dough on a lightly floured surface to a thickness of about ⅛ inch. Using a sharp knife, cut the dough into twelve 4½-by-3½-inch rectangles, and use these to line oval tartlet pans measuring approximately 3 by 2 by ¾ inches. Prick the inside surfaces all over with a fork and chill the cases for 30 minutes.

Bake the cases until they are lightly browned—15 to 20 minutes. Remove the cases from the oven, cool them slightly, and unmold them onto a wire rack.

In the meantime, prepare the wine syrup. Put the wine, sugar, and orange zest into a small, nonreactive saucepan, and heat on low, stirring with a wooden spoon, until the sugar has dissolved. Bring the mixture almost to a boil, then remove it from the heat and allow it to stand, covered, for approximately 30 minutes, so that the syrup becomes infused with the flavor of the orange zest.

Using a slotted spoon, remove the orange zest from the syrup. Sprinkle the gelatin over 2 tablespoons of water in a small bowl, and let it soften for two minutes. Set the bowl over a pan of simmering water and stir until the gelatin has fully dissolved. Whisk the warm gelatin into the wine mixture, then chill the syrup until it just begins to set—about 30 minutes.

Cut the grapes in half. Place 1 teaspoon of sour cream in each pastry case, arrange 4 grape halves on top, then pour a little of the wine syrup over them, shaking the tartlets gently to encourage the syrup to fill the spaces between the grapes. Brush any remaining syrup over the surface of the grapes. Chill the tartlets until the filling is set—20 to 30 minutes—then serve them as soon as possible.

Fig Flowers

Makes 16 flowers
Working time: about 40 minutes
Total time: about 1 hour and 20 minutes

Per flower:
Calories **105**
Protein **2g.**
Cholesterol **trace**
Total fat **7g.**
Saturated fat **1g.**
Sodium **80mg.**

1¼ cups unbleached all-purpose flour
¼ cup cornmeal
1 tsp. sugar
6 tbsp. polyunsaturated margarine, chilled
1 egg white
Creamy fig filling
5 ripe figs, quartered lengthwise
4 oz. low-fat cream cheese
1 tbsp. plain low-fat yogurt
1 tsp. rose water (optional)
1 tsp. sugar

To make the dough, sift the flour, cornmeal, and sugar into a mixing bowl; using your fintertips or the back of a wooden spoon, rub in the margarine until the mixture resembles fine breadcrumbs. Mix in the egg white with a wooden spoon, then gather the dough into a ball and knead it briefly on a lightly floured surface until smooth.

Preheat the oven to 375° F.

Roll the dough out to a thickness of about ⅛ inch, and cut out 16 shapes with a 3-inch flower cutter. Fit the shapes into 3-inch tartlet pans, easing the dough across the bottom and up the sides of the pans without spoiling the petals. Prick the inside surfaces with a fork and chill the cases for 30 minutes.

Bake the tartlet cases until they are lightly browned around the edges—7 to 10 minutes. Allow the cases to cool slightly, then turn them out onto a wire rack to cool completely.

To fill the tartlets, cut the fig quarters lengthwise into thin slices, and arrange the slices in the pastry flowers to look like petals. Using a wooden spoon, beat together the cream cheese, yogurt, rose water, if you are using it, and sugar until the mixture becomes smooth and creamy. Transfer the mixture to a pastry bag fitted with a ¼-inch star tip, and pipe a mound of filling into the center of each flower.

Orange Tartlets

Makes 24 tartlets
Working time: about 1 hour
Total time: about 2 hours

Per tartlet:
Calories **90**
Protein **2g.**
Cholesterol **20mg.**
Total fat **5g.**
Saturated fat **1g.**
Sodium **45mg.**

9 oz. shortcrust dough (recipe, page 10)
1¼ cups orange-flavored pastry cream (recipe, page 11)
4 oranges, zest and pith cut off, segmented (technique, page 41), segments halved lengthwise, 1 tbsp. juice reserved
1 tbsp. orange marmalade, strained
1 oz. pistachio nuts, peeled and thinly sliced (about ¼ cup)

Preheat the oven to 425° F. Roll out the dough on a lightly floured surface to a thickness of about ⅛ inch. Using a 2¾-inch fluted cutter, cut out rounds from the dough, and use these to line twenty-four 2½-inch tartlet pans or muffin pans. (The rounds of dough do not completely fill the pans because the tartlets should be shallow.) Using a fork, lightly prick the inside surfaces of the cases and refrigerate them for 30 minutes.

Bake the chilled pastry cases until they are lightly browned—15 to 20 minutes. Allow them to cool a little in the pans, then unmold them onto wire racks to cool completely.

Spoon or pipe the pastry cream into the tartlet cases, then arrange the orange slices neatly on top. Put the reserved orange juice into a small, nonreactive saucepan with the orange marmalade. Heat the mixture over low heat until it comes to a boil. Cook it for one minute, then use a pastry brush to spread the glaze evenly over the orange segments. Sprinkle the tartlets with the pistachio nuts.

The tartlets may be served in trimmed-down paper baking cases. Serve them the day they are prepared.

EDITOR'S NOTE: *To peel pistachio nuts, blanch them in boiling water for one minute, drain them thoroughly, then rub them vigorously in a dishtowel.*

Cherry Custard Tartlets

Makes 12 tartlets
Working time: about 20 minutes
Total time: about 1 hour and 10 minutes

Per tartlet:
Calories **95**
Protein **2g.**
Cholesterol **15mg.**
Total fat **5g.**
Saturated fat **2g.**
Sodium **50mg.**

9 oz. shortcrust dough (recipe, page 10)
1 egg
1 tbsp. sugar
⅛ tsp. ground cinnamon
5 tbsp. light cream
2 tbsp. skim milk
24 sweet cherries (about 6 oz.), pitted

Preheat the oven to 425° F. On a lightly floured surface, roll out the dough to a thickness of ¼ inch. Cut out 12 circles with a 4-inch cutter, and use them to line deep 2½-inch tartlet pans. Prick the inside surfaces with a fork, then chill the tartlet cases for 30 minutes.

Arrange the tartlet cases on a baking sheet and bake them for five minutes. Prepare the custard filling by whisking together the egg, sugar, cinnamon, cream, and skim milk.

Remove the baking sheet from the oven. Put two cherries into each tartlet case, then pour in the custard mixture. Return the tartlets to the oven, and bake them until the custard is set and just beginning to brown—about 20 minutes. Serve them warm or cold.

Lemon Meringue Barquettes

Makes 20 barquettes
Working time: about 1 hour
Total time: about 2 hours and 30 minutes
(includes chilling)

Per barquette:
Calories **110**
Protein **2g.**
Cholesterol **15mg.**
Total fat **4g.**
Saturated fat **1g.**
Sodium **45mg.**

9 oz. shortcrust dough (recipe, page 10)
Lemon filling
2 lemons, zest thinly pared, juice strained
⅓ cup cornstarch
2 tbsp. sugar
1 egg yolk
Meringue topping
¼ cup sugar
7 tbsp. confectioners' sugar
2 egg whites

First, begin preparing the filling. Put the lemon zest into a nonreactive saucepan with 1¼ cups of water. Bring the liquid to a boil, then remove the saucepan from the heat. Cover the pan and allow the liquid to stand for at least 30 minutes, so that it becomes infused with the flavor of the lemon zest.

Preheat the oven to 425° F. On a lightly floured surface, roll out the dough to a thickness of about ⅛ inch. Cut the dough into twenty 5-by-2¾-inch rectangles, and use these to line 4-by-1¾-inch barquette molds. Lightly prick the inside surface of each case all over with a fork, then chill the cases for 30 minutes.

Bake the barquette cases until the pastry is very lightly browned—20 to 25 minutes. Allow the cases to cool a little in their molds, then carefully unmold them onto a large baking sheet. Set them aside while you complete the filling. Leave the oven on.

Using a slotted spoon, remove the lemon zest from the saucepan, then stir in the lemon juice. In a small bowl, blend the cornstarch with a little of the lemon liquid to form a smooth cream, then stir it into the saucepan. Bring the mixture to a boil, stirring continuously until it thickens and clears. Continue cooking over low heat for two to three minutes more. Remove the saucepan from the heat, then beat the sugar and egg yolk into the lemon mixture. Spoon the lemon filling into the barquette cases, filling them to just below their tops.

To make the meringue topping, sift both kinds of sugar into a bowl. In a separate bowl, whisk the egg whites until they are stiff but not dry. Gradually beat the sugar into the egg whites, 1 level tablespoon at a time, beating well between each addition to make a stiff, shiny meringue.

Spoon the meringue into a pastry bag fitted with a ⅓-inch star tip, and pipe the meringue decoratively on top of the lemon filling in each pastry case. Alternatively, spoon on the meringue, smoothing it with the back of a teaspoon. Bake the barquettes until the meringue just begins to turn light brown—four to five minutes. Allow the barquettes to cool, then refrigerate them for 30 minutes before serving.

Lemon Curd Tartlets

Makes 18 tartlets
Working time: about 35 minutes
Total time: about 1 hour and 15 minutes

Per tartlet:
Calories **125**
Protein **3g.**
Cholesterol **15mg.**
Total fat **10g.**
Saturated fat **2g.**
Sodium **110mg.**

9 oz. shortcrust dough (recipe, page 10)
⅔ cup part-skim ricotta cheese
1 lemon, grated zest only
1½ tbsp. fresh lemon juice
1½ tbsp. honey
1 egg, lightly beaten
1 egg white
2 tbsp. fresh breadcrumbs
½ oz. sliced almonds
Sugar icing
½ lightly beaten egg white
7 tbsp. confectioners' sugar, sifted

On a lightly floured surface, roll out the dough to a thickness of about ⅛ inch. Using a 3-inch cutter, cut out 18 circles, and use these to line 2½-inch tartlet molds or muffin pans. (The rounds of dough do not completely fill the pans because the tartlets should be shallow.) Prick the inside surfaces with a fork, then chill the tartlet cases for 15 minutes.

Preheat the oven to 400° F.

In the meantime, make the filling. Beat the ricotta cheese with the lemon zest and juice and the honey, then mix in the whole egg, egg white, and breadcrumbs. Spoon this mixture into the chilled pastry cases, filling them two-thirds full. Sprinkle a few almond slices over the top of each.

To make the icing, mix the egg white and confectioners' sugar together until smooth, then spoon a little over each tartlet. Bake the tartlets until they are risen and golden—about 20 minutes. Unmold the tartlets onto a wire rack, and allow them to cool for 10 to 15 minutes before serving.

Red-Currant Meringue Squares

Makes 24 squares
Working time: about 40 minutes
Total time: about 4 hours and 30 minutes

Per square:	
Calories **90**	9 oz. shortcrust dough (recipe, page 10)
Protein **1g.**	1½ lb. red currants, picked over, or cherries, pitted
Cholesterol **0mg.**	¾ cup sugar
Total fat **3g.**	1 tbsp. cornstarch
Saturated fat **1g.**	2 egg whites
Sodium **40mg.**	

Preheat the oven to 425° F.

Roll out the dough into a rectangle on a lightly floured surface, and trim it to line the bottom of a 13-by-9-inch baking pan. Lift the dough on a rolling pin and ease it into the bottom of the pan, pressing it down gently. Prick the dough with the tines of a fork and chill it for 30 minutes.

Bake the pastry until it is lightly browned—20 to 25 minutes. Remove it from the oven and lower the oven temperature to 160° F.

Put the red currants or cherries and half of the sugar into a nonreactive saucepan. Cook over low heat until the fruit is soft and the mixture is liquid—four to five minutes. Blend the cornstarch with 1 tablespoon of water, stirring to form a smooth paste. Add the cornstarch paste to the fruit, bring to a boil, and cook, stirring, until the mixture thickens and becomes translucent—about two minutes. Spread the fruit mixture over the pastry base.

Beat the egg whites until they form peaks, then gradually whip in the remaining sugar until the mixture is stiff and glossy. Transfer the meringue to a pastry bag fitted with a ⅓-inch star tip, and pipe a diagonal lattice pattern over the fruit. Bake the tart for two hours, then turn off the heat and allow the tart to cool inside the oven.

Cut the tart into twenty-four 2-inch-square pieces before serving.

Cranberry Meringue Tartlets

Makes 18 tartlets
Working time: about 1 hour
Total time: about 2 hours

Per tartlet:
Calories **115**
Protein **2g.**
Cholesterol **0mg.**
Total fat **4g.**
Saturated fat **1g.**
Sodium **50mg.**

9 oz. shortcrust dough (recipe, page 10)
Fruit filling
6 oz. fresh cranberries, picked over, or frozen cranberries, thawed
3 tbsp. fresh orange juice
2 tbsp. honey
2 tbsp. sugar
½ tsp. arrowroot dissolved in 2 tsp. cold water
Meringue topping
2 egg whites
½ cup sugar

Preheat the oven to 425° F. On a lightly floured surface, roll out the dough to a thickness of about ⅛ inch. Using a 3-inch cutter, stamp out 18 rounds, and use these to line 2½-inch tartlet pans. Prick the inside surfaces with a fork, and chill the cases for 30 minutes.

Stand the pans on a baking sheet, and bake the pastry cases until they are lightly browned and crisp—15 to 20 minutes. Allow the cases to cool in the pans slightly, then unmold them onto a baking sheet. Lower the oven temperature to 300° F.

While the pastry cases are baking, make the fruit filling. Put the cranberries into a small, nonreactive saucepan with the orange juice, and cook over low heat, covered, until the fruit is soft and all the cranberries have popped—about eight minutes. Stir in the honey and sugar, then add the arrowroot. Bring the mixture to a boil, stirring until it has thickened, then remove the pan from the heat and allow the filling to cool. Spoon the cooled cranberry mixture into the pastry cases.

To make the topping, beat the egg whites until they form peaks, then whip in the sugar, a tablespoon at a time, until the meringue is stiff and glossy. Transfer the meringue to a pastry bag fitted with a ½-inch star tip, and pipe a whirl on top of each tart to completely cover the filling. Return the tartlets to the oven and bake them until the meringue is tinged a pale brown—about 10 minutes.

Cherry Bakewell Barquettes

THIS RECIPE IS IDEAL FOR USING UP SPONGE-CAKE TRIMMINGS.

Makes 30 barquettes
Working time: about 1 hour
Total time: about 1 hour and 40 minutes

Per barquette:
Calories **95**
Protein **1g.**
Cholesterol **10mg.**
Total fat **5g.**
Saturated fat **1g.**
Sodium **50mg.**

9 oz. shortcrust dough (recipe, page 10)
4 tbsp. red jam (raspberry, strawberry, or black cherry) without added sugar
3 tbsp. apricot jam without added sugar
4 candied cherries, finely chopped
2 tbsp. pine nuts, lightly toasted
Almond filling
4 tbsp. polyunsaturated margarine
2 tbsp. sugar
½ tsp. pure almond extract
1 egg, beaten
6 tbsp. sponge-cake crumbs
¼ cup ground almonds

Roll out the dough on a lightly floured surface to a thickness of about ⅛ inch. Cut out thirty 4-by-2-inch rectangles and use these to line 3½-by-1½-inch barquette molds. Press the dough firmly into the molds and trim the edges. Place the barquette cases on a baking sheet and chill them for 30 minutes.

In the meantime, preheat the oven to 425° F. and prepare the filling. Put the margarine and sugar together into a small mixing bowl, and beat well until the mixture is smooth and creamy. Beat in the almond extract, then gradually beat in the egg. Add the sponge-cake crumbs and ground almonds, and fold them in lightly.

Put a little red jam—slightly less than half a teaspoonful—into each barquette case and spread it evenly over the bottom. Spoon the filling on top of the jam—each case should be three-quarters full—and smooth the tops. Bake until the filling is well risen, golden brown, and firm to the touch—15 to 20 minutes. Allow the barquettes to cool slightly in the molds, then unmold them onto wire racks to cool completely.

In a small pan, bring the apricot jam to a boil, press it through a fine sieve to remove any solids, then brush it lightly over each barquette. Arrange chopped cherries and pine nuts on top of the glaze.

EDITOR'S NOTE: *These barquettes may be stored in an airtight container for two to three days. Toast pine nuts in a 350° F. oven until they are golden—four to five minutes. Toss the nuts after two to three minutes so that they color evenly.*

Honey and Hazelnut Tartlets

Makes 10 tartlets
Working time: about 25 minutes
Total time: about 1 hour and 5 minutes

Per tartlet:	
Calories **102**	5 oz. shortcrust dough (recipe, page 10)
Protein **2g.**	¼ cup sugar
Cholesterol **10mg.**	2 tbsp. honey
Total fat **11g.**	2 tbsp. unsalted butter
Saturated fat **2g.**	1 cup hazelnuts, toasted and
Sodium **70mg.**	peeled (box, below)

Preheat the oven to 425° F.

Roll out the dough on a lightly floured surface to a thickness of about ⅛ inch. Using a 3-inch cutter, cut out 10 circles and use these to line 2½-inch tartlet molds. Prick the inside surfaces with the tines of a fork, place the molds on a baking sheet, and put them into the refrigerator to chill for 30 minutes.

Bake the pastry cases until they are golden brown— 15 to 20 minutes. Remove them from the oven, allow them to cool a little in the molds, then unmold the tartlet cases onto a wire rack.

To make the filling, place the sugar, honey, and 1 tablespoon of water in a small, heavy-bottomed sauce-pan over low heat. Stir the mixture until all the sugar has completely dissolved; if any sugar crystals have stuck to the sides of the pan, brush them down with a pastry brush dipped in warm water. Warm a candy thermometer in hot water, then place it in the syrup. Increase the heat to high and bring the syrup to a boil. Boil it rapidly until the temperature on the thermometer registers between 223° F. and 234° F.; the syrup will form a fine, short thread when dripped from a spoon. Remove the saucepan from the heat, and stir in the butter and hazelnuts.

Spoon the mixture into the pastry cases, and allow the tartlets to cool and set before serving.

Peeling Hazelnuts

1 TOASTING AND PEELING THE NUTS. Place the hazelnuts on a baking sheet in a preheated 350° F. oven for about 10 minutes. Lay a towel on a work surface and tip the nuts onto it. Fold the towel over the nuts, and using the palms of your hands, vigorously roll the nuts. After one or two minutes, most nuts will have shed their skins.

2 REMOVING STUBBORN SKINS. Rub any unpeeled or partly peeled nuts between your fingers so that the skin flakes off. Nuts enclosed in their skins even after being rubbed should be reserved for occasions when appearance is not important. Store the nuts in an airtight container if you are not using them immediately.

Rum and Raisin Tartlets

Makes 18 tartlets
Working time: about 35 minutes
Total time: about 6 hours (includes soaking)

Per tartlet:
Calories **125**
Protein **2g.**
Cholesterol **25mg.**
Total fat **5g.**
Saturated fat **1g.**
Sodium **45mg.**

9 oz. shortcrust dough (recipe, page 10)
1 orange, zest only, cut into fine shreds with a zester
Rum and raisin filling
⅔ cup raisins
2 tbsp. white rum
2 eggs, separated
6 tbsp. light brown sugar
2 tsp. unbleached all-purpose flour
¼ tsp. ground cinnamon
½ cup plain low-fat yogurt

First, begin preparing the filling. Put the raisins and white rum into a small saucepan, cover, and heat on low for two to three minutes. Remove the pan from the heat and let the raisins soak for at least four hours, or preferably overnight.

Preheat the oven to 400° F.

Roll out the dough on a lightly floured surface to a thickness of about ⅛ inch. Using a 3-inch cutter, cut out 18 circles, and use these to line 2½-inch tartlet pans. Prick the inside surfaces with a fork and chill the pastry cases for 30 minutes.

Place the tartlet pans on a baking sheet, and bake the cases until they are crisp and light brown—about 15 minutes. Remove the tartlets from the oven and set them aside to cool while you complete the filling. Lower the oven temperature to 350° F.

In a large bowl, beat the egg yolks with 4 table-spoons of the sugar until the mixture is thick and pale. In a separate bowl, beat the egg whites until they form soft peaks, then sprinkle in the remaining sugar and whip until the whites are stiff and glossy. Sift the flour and cinnamon over the beaten egg yolks, add one-third of the egg whites and one-third of the yogurt, and fold all the ingredients in quickly and lightly until the mixture is evenly blended. Add another third of the egg whites and yogurt in the same way, followed by the last third. Fold in the raisins, then fill the tartlet cases with the mixture, making sure that the raisins are evenly distributed.

Bake the tartlets until they are lightly browned and just firm to the touch—20 to 25 minutes. Transfer the tartlets to a wire rack to cool, and decorate them with shreds of orange zest before serving.

Chocolate Slices

Makes 8 slices
Working time: about 1 hour
Total time: about 3 hours and 30 minutes (includes chilling)

Per slice:
Calories **240**
Protein **9g.**
Cholesterol **10mg.**
Total fat **12g.**
Saturated fat **5g.**
Sodium **240mg.**

1 cup unbleached all-purpose flour
1 tsp. sugar
4 tbsp. polyunsaturated margarine, chilled
1 tbsp. cocoa powder
3 egg whites
8 oz. low-fat cream cheese
6 tbsp. sour cream
2 tbsp. honey
2 tsp. powdered gelatin
3½ oz. semisweet chocolate

To make the pastry, sift the flour and sugar into a mixing bowl, then rub in the margarine with your fingertips until the mixture resembles fine breadcrumbs. Stir in the cocoa powder and 1 of the egg whites, and mix with a wooden spoon to form a dough. Gather the dough into a ball and knead it briefly on a lightly floured surface until smooth.

Preheat the oven to 425° F. Roll out the dough to a thickness of about ⅛ inch, and use it to line the bottom of a 6-inch-square pan with a removable bottom—the pan should be at least 1½ inches deep. (If you do not have a pan with a removable bottom, you may line the pan with foil, being careful to press the foil into the corners.) Press the dough well into the corners, prick it all over with a fork, then chill for 30 minutes.

Bake the pastry until it is crisp and brown—15 to 20 minutes—then remove it from the oven and allow it to cool in the pan.

To make the filling, place the cream cheese, sour cream, and 1 tablespoon of the honey in a mixing bowl. Whip until smooth. Sprinkle the gelatin over 2 tablespoons of water in a small bowl, and let it soften for two minutes. Set the bowl over a saucepan of gently simmering water and stir until the gelatin has completely dissolved. Gradually pour the dissolved gelatin into the cream-cheese mixture, beating well.

Break up the chocolate and reserve one-quarter of it. Place the remainder in a bowl set over a saucepan of hot but not boiling water, and heat until the chocolate is melted. Divide the cream-cheese mixture between two bowls. Beat the melted chocolate into one bowl, and beat the remaining tablespoon of honey into the other. In another bowl, beat the remaining egg whites until they form soft peaks; using a tablespoon, fold half into the chocolate mixture and half into the honey mixture.

Line the sides of the pan with parchment paper. Spoon the chocolate mixture over the pastry and level the surface. Spread the honey mixture over the chocolate layer, then chill until firm—about two hours.

When the filling has set, mark the surface into eight sections. Melt the reserved chocolate as above, and place it in a wax-paper or parchment-paper pastry bag, folded as shown on page 13. Pipe decorative designs over the individual marked sections.

Just before serving, carefully lift the assembly out of the pan, peel off the paper, and cut into eight slices.

Blackberry and Almond Boats

Makes 16 boats
Working time: about 40 minutes
Total time: about 1 hour and 35 minutes

Per boat:
Calories **150**
Protein **2g.**
Cholesterol **trace**
Total fat **7g.**
Saturated fat **1g.**
Sodium **55mg.**

9 oz. shortcrust dough (recipe, page 10)
2 tsp. confectioners' sugar
Blackberry filling
8 oz. fresh blackberries
1 tbsp. arrowroot
2 tbsp. sugar
Almond topping
2 egg whites
7 tbsp. vanilla sugar, or 7 tbsp. sugar mixed with ½ tsp. pure vanilla extract
⅔ cup ground almonds

First, prepare the blackberry filling. Press the blackberries through a fine sieve into a nonreactive saucepan. Blend the arrowroot with 1 tablespoon of cold water, then stir it into the puréed blackberries. Bring the purée to a boil, stirring continuously; boil until the mixture thickens and clears. Continue to cook the purée over low heat until the arrowroot is cooked—three to four minutes. Stir in the sugar, then let the purée cool for about 20 minutes while you roll out the shortcrust dough.

Preheat the oven to 425° F. Roll out the dough on a lightly floured surface to a thickness of about ⅛ inch. Cut the dough into sixteen 5-by-2¾-inch rectangles, and use these to line 4-by-1¾-inch fluted barquette molds, pressing the dough well into the flutes. Trim the edges and place the molds on a baking sheet. Divide the cooled fruit purée equally among the lined molds, spreading it evenly.

To make the almond topping, beat the egg whites to obtain a froth of small, uniform bubbles, then beat in the vanilla sugar. Fold in the ground almonds. Put the mixture into a pastry bag fitted with a ¼-inch plain tip. Pipe the almond mixture evenly to cover the surface of the blackberry purée.

Bake the tarts until the topping is well risen and golden brown—20 to 25 minutes; they will probably develop a slight crack in the center. Allow the tarts to cool in their pans for about five minutes, then carefully turn them out onto a wire rack. When the tarts are cool, sift confectioners' sugar very lightly over them.

SUGGESTED ACCOMPANIMENT: *fresh blackberries.*

Souffléed Coffee Diamonds

Makes 10 diamonds
Working time: about 40 minutes
Total time: about 3 hours (includes chilling)

Per diamond:
Calories **170**
Protein **3g.**
Cholesterol **30mg.**
Total fat **11g.**
Saturated fat **4g.**
Sodium **100mg.**

1½ cups unbleached all-purpose flour
6 tbsp. polyunsaturated margarine, chilled
2 tbsp. dark brown sugar
½ tbsp. cocoa powder
Coffee soufflé
1 egg yolk
3 tbsp. light brown sugar
3 tbsp. strong black coffee
1 tsp. powdered gelatin
2 egg whites
6 tbsp. whipping cream

To make the diamond cases, sift the flour into a mixing bowl. Rub in the margarine with your fingertips until the mixture resembles fine breadcrumbs, then stir in the sugar. Add 2 teaspoons of cold water and mix with a wooden spoon to form a firm dough. Gather the dough into a ball and knead it briefly on a lightly floured surface until it is smooth.

Roll out the dough to a thickness of about ⅛ inch, and using a sharp knife, cut out ten 4½-by-3½-inch diamonds. Use these to line 3½-by-2½-inch diamond-shaped tartlet molds, pressing the dough firmly into

the contours of the mold. Prick the insides with a fork, then put the tartlet molds on a baking sheet and chill for 30 minutes. Meanwhile, reroll the trimmings and cut out 30 small leaves. Using the tip of a sharp knife, etch a leaf pattern onto the surface of each. Place the leaves on a baking sheet and chill with the cases.

Preheat the oven to 425° F. Bake the leaves for about three minutes and the cases for 15 to 20 minutes—they should be crisp and light brown. Let the cases cool slightly in the molds, then unmold them onto a rack, together with the leaves, to finish cooling.

To make the coffee soufflé, place the egg yolk in a bowl with the sugar and black coffee. Beat until the mixture is pale and frothy—about five minutes. Sprinkle the gelatin over 2 tablespoons of water in a small bowl, and let it soften for two minutes. Set the bowl over a saucepan of simmering water, and stir until the gelatin has completely dissolved. Gradually pour the dissolved gelatin into the coffee mixture, beating well.

Chill the mixture until it has almost set—about 30 minutes. Beat the egg whites until they are stiff, and whip the cream until it holds soft peaks. Using a tablespoon, fold the cream, then the egg whites, into the coffee mixture. Chill until lightly set—about one hour.

Spoon the soufflé into a pastry bag fitted with a large star tip, and pipe swirls into the pastry cases. Sprinkle the diamonds with the cocoa powder and decorate them with the pastry leaves. Chill for at least another 30 minutes before serving.

Chocolate Puffs with Strawberry Mousse

Makes 12 puffs
Working time: about 30 minutes
Total time: about 1 hour and 30 minutes
(includes chilling)

Per puff: Calories **125** Protein **8g.** Cholesterol **50mg.** Total fat **10g.** Saturated fat **4g.** Sodium **25mg.**	*chou-puff dough (recipe, page 10), substituting 1 tbsp.* *of cocoa powder for 2 tbsp. of the flour*
	1 tbsp. confectioners' sugar
	Strawberry mousse
	2 tsp. powdered gelatin
	1¾ cups strawberries, hulled
	¾ cup part-skim ricotta cheese
	1 tbsp. sugar
	1 tsp. kirsch or eau de vie framboise

Preheat the oven to 425° F.

To make the mousse, first sprinkle the powdered gelatin over 2 tablespoons of water in a small bowl and set it aside to allow it to soften—about two minutes. While the gelatin softens, process 1 cup of the strawberries in a food processor or a blender with the ricotta cheese, sugar, and kirsch or *eau de vie*. Place the bowl of gelatin over a pan of simmering water and stir until the gelatin has dissolved. Add the dissolved gelatin to the strawberry mixture and process for 20 seconds more. Then transfer the mousse mixture to a bowl and refrigerate until the mousse is set—approximately one hour.

In the meantime, line a baking sheet with parchment paper and drop 12 rounded tablespoons of the prepared dough onto it, spaced well apart, to make puffs. Bake until the choux are well risen and firm—25 to 30 minutes. Using the tip of a sharp knife, pierce a few small holes in the sides of each puff to allow the steam to escape. Return the puffs to the oven for five minutes more to dry out, then transfer them to a wire rack to cool.

Slice the puffs in half, remove any uncooked dough from the centers, then pipe or spoon the set mousse into the bases. Finely slice the remaining strawberries and arrange the slices on top of the mousse. Replace the puff tops, lightly dust them with confectioners' sugar, and serve. The puffs will hold the filling for about two hours before they start to go soft.

Raspberry-Almond Rings on Shortcrust

Makes 28 rings
Working time: about 50 minutes
Total time: about 1 hour and 15 minutes

Per ring: Calories **90** Protein **2g.** Cholesterol **40mg.** Total fat **6g.** Saturated fat **2g.** Sodium **60mg.**	*9 oz. shortcrust dough (recipe, page 10)*
	2 oz. sliced almonds
	2 cups orange-flavored pastry cream (recipe, page 11)
	1½ cups fresh raspberries
	1 tbsp. confectioners' sugar
	Chou-puff dough
	3 tbsp. unsalted butter
	¼ cup unbleached all-purpose flour
	1 egg
	1 egg white

Roll out the shortcrust dough on a lightly floured surface to a thickness of about ⅛ inch. Prick it well with a fork. Using a 3-inch plain cutter, cut out rounds from the dough and place them on baking sheets. Reroll the trimmings and stamp out more rounds until you have 28 in all. Refrigerate the rounds while you make the chou-puff dough.

Preheat the oven to 400° F.

Make the chou-puff dough according to the method on page 10, using ½ cup of water and the ingredients listed above. Transfer the dough to a pastry bag fitted with a ¼-inch plain tip. Pipe a ring of dough onto each chilled shortcrust round, about ⅛ inch in from the edge. Arrange the sliced almonds evenly over the

choux. Bake the rings until they are well risen, golden brown, and crisp—15 to 20 minutes. Transfer the pastries to wire racks to cool.

Fill the centers with the orange-flavored pastry cream and top the filling with the raspberries. Sift the confectioners' sugar lightly over the finished rings.

EDITOR'S NOTE: *Small strawberries, blackberries, red currants, or black currants can be substituted for the raspberries.*

Peach Puffs

TRAPPING STEAM TO COOK THE CHOUX PRODUCES
A VERY LARGE, CRISP-TOPPED PUFF FROM ONLY A SMALL
AMOUNT OF DOUGH.

Makes 4 puffs
Working time: about 35 minutes
Total time: about 3 hours and 15 minutes
(includes chilling)

Per puff:
Calories **150**
Protein **5g.**
Cholesterol **75mg.**
Total fat **9g.**
Saturated fat **4g.**
Sodium **25mg.**

Peach filling
½ cup fresh orange juice
1 tsp. powdered gelatin
2 tsp. orange-flavored liqueur (optional)
1 large peach
3 tbsp. sour cream
Chou-puff dough
2 tbsp. unsalted butter
⅓ cup unbleached all-purpose flour
1 egg

First, make the filling. Put 1 tablespoon of the orange juice into a small bowl, sprinkle on the gelatin, and allow it to soften for two minutes. Set the bowl over a pan of gently simmering water and stir until the gelatin has fully dissolved. In a mixing bowl, stir the gelatin mixture and the liqueur, if you are using it, into the rest of the orange juice. Chill the mixture until it just begins to set—about one hour—while you prepare and cook the chou-puff dough.

Preheat the oven to 425° F. Grease a baking sheet and find two large loaf pans, or similar pans, that will sit flat and give a good seal when inverted onto the baking sheet.

Following the method on page 10, make the chou-puff dough with 5 tablespoons of water and the ingredients listed at left. Divide the dough into four equal portions, and place the dough on the baking sheet, positioned so that each loaf pan can cover two puffs. Set the loaf pans over the puffs and bake until the puffs move on the baking sheet when the covering pan is gently shaken—35 to 40 minutes. Carefully remove the covering pans and transfer the puffs to a wire rack to cool.

Skin the peach by dipping it briefly into a pan of boiling water and then into a bowl of cold water; the skin should slip off easily. Chop the peach flesh, add it to the partially set jelly, then chill again until the mixture is firmly set—about two hours.

Just before serving, assemble the puffs. Cut the tops off the puffs and divide the jellied peaches between the bases. Top the peaches with a dollop of sour cream and replace the lids.

Tricorn Puffs

Makes 14 puffs
Working time: about 50 minutes
Total time: about 1 hour and 50 minutes

Per puff:
Calories **160**
Protein **5g.**
Cholesterol **75mg.**
Total fat **8g.**
Saturated fat **4g.**
Sodium **50mg.**

chou-puff dough (recipe, page 10)
1¼ cups pastry cream (recipe, page 11)
½ lb. seedless green or red grapes, or a mixture of both, stemmed
2 tbsp. apricot jam or orange marmalade
2 oz. slivered almonds, toasted

Preheat the oven to 425° F. Line three baking sheets with parchment paper.

Place the chou-puff dough in a pastry bag fitted with a ⅝-inch plain tip. Make 14 tricorns on the prepared baking sheets by piping three balls of dough for each one, with the balls touching to make a triangle shape. Bake the tricorns until the pastry is well risen, golden brown, and crisp—25 to 30 minutes. Remove the puffs from the oven, and use the tip of a sharp knife to pierce a small hole in the side of each. Return the tricorns to the oven for five minutes more to dry them out, then transfer them to wire racks to cool.

Split the puffs in half and remove any uncooked dough from the centers. Fill the bases with the pastry cream and a few grapes; if the grapes are large, halve or quarter them first. Replace the tricorn tops. Heat the jam or marmalade in a small saucepan until it becomes liquid, sieve it to remove any solids, then use a pastry brush to spread a little over the top of each puff. Sprinkle on a few toasted almond slivers and serve within one hour.

EDITOR'S NOTE: *To toast slivered almonds, put them under the broiler until they become golden—about two minutes; turn or shake them constantly.*

Fresh Fruit Galette

Makes 16 slices
Working time: about 1 hour and 40 minutes
Total time: about 3 hours and 15 minutes
(includes chilling)

Per slice:
Calories **220**
Protein **4g.**
Cholesterol **50mg.**
Total fat **8g.**
Saturated fat **4g.**
Sodium **75mg.**

1¼ cups liqueur-flavored pastry cream (recipe, page 11), made with orange-flavored liqueur and 1 egg yolk instead of 2
1¾ cups strawberries, hulled and sliced
2 kiwi fruit, peeled, halved lengthwise, and sliced
12 oz. fresh pineapple, peeled, quartered, cored, and sliced
12 black grapes, halved and seeds removed
2 large peaches, halved, pitted, and sliced
2 tsp. confectioners' sugar
½ cup white wine
¼ cup sugar
2 tbsp. orange-flavored liqueur

Rich shortcrust base

1¼ cups unbleached all-purpose flour
1½ tbsp. confectioners' sugar
5 tbsp. unsalted butter, chilled
1 egg yolk, lightly beaten

Chou-puff dough

3 tbsp. unsalted butter
½ cup unbleached all-purpose flour
1 egg
1 egg white
a little beaten egg white for brushing

First, make the shortcrust base. Sift the flour and sugar into a bowl. Rub in the butter with your fingertips until the mixture resembles fine breadcrumbs, then make a well in the center. Add the egg yolk and 5 teaspoons of ice water, then mix with a wooden spoon to form a fairly stiff dough. Knead the dough very lightly on a floured surface until smooth, then cover it tightly with plastic wrap and refrigerate it for 30 minutes.

Roll out the dough on a lightly floured surface into a square a little larger than 12 inches. Trim the square to exactly 12 inches. Prick the dough well with a fork, then cut it in half to make two equal rectangles. Place the rectangles on one large or two small baking sheets. Refrigerate them for 30 minutes.

Preheat the oven to 400° F. Prepare the chou-puff dough according to the method on page 10, using ½ cup of water and the first four ingredients listed above.

Put the dough into a pastry bag fitted with a ½-inch 12-point star tip. Brush a ½-inch-wide strip of beaten egg white down each long side of the chilled rectangles of shortcrust dough. Carefully pipe an even single line of chou-puff dough on top of the egg white, about ¼ inch in from the edge.

Bake the assembled galette bases until the chou-puff dough is well risen, golden brown, and firm to the touch—about 25 minutes. Using the tip of a small, sharp knife, make several incisions along the inside edge of each chou strip to allow the steam to escape. Return the galette bases to the oven for five minutes, then carefully transfer them to wire racks to cool.

Slice the chou strips in half horizontally and scoop out any uncooked dough. Fit a pastry bag with a ½-inch 12-point star tip, and fill it with the pastry cream. Pipe a line of cream filling into each chou strip, and replace the tops. Spread the remaining pastry cream in an even layer over the shortcrust base, between the chou strips. Arrange the strawberries, kiwi fruit, pineapple, grapes, and peaches in neat lines on top of the pastry cream. Sift the confectioners' sugar lightly over the chou-puff borders.

Finally, make a glaze for the fruit. Put the wine, sugar, and liqueur into a small saucepan. Heat on low, stirring, until the sugar dissolves, then boil the syrup until it is reduced and syrupy—three to four minutes. Brush the glaze evenly over the fruit.

Cut each galette into eight slices for serving. The galette should be served on the day of preparation.

Raspberry Whole-Wheat Puffs

Makes 12 puffs
Working time: about 25 minutes
Total time: about 1 hour and 10 minutes

Per puff:
Calories **95**
Protein **3g.**
Cholesterol **50mg.**
Total fat **6g.**
Saturated fat **3g.**
Sodium **100mg.**

4 tbsp. unsalted butter
⅓ cup whole-wheat flour, sifted, bran reserved
¼ cup unbleached all-purpose flour, sifted
2 eggs, lightly beaten
1 tsp. sesame seeds
1 tbsp. confectioners' sugar
Raspberry-cheese filling
½ cup part-skim ricotta cheese
1 tbsp. honey
4 oz. fresh raspberries

Preheat the oven to 400° F. Line a large baking sheet with parchment paper.

Put the butter and ½ cup of water into a heavy-bottomed saucepan, and heat on low until the butter melts. Increase the heat to medium high and bring the liquid to a boil. Remove the pan from the heat, add the two types of flour and the bran all at once, and beat vigorously with a wooden spoon. Return the pan to the heat and continue beating until the mixture forms a ball in the center of the pan. Allow the mixture to cool for a few minutes.

Set aside 1 tablespoon of the beaten egg. Using an electric hand-held mixer, beat the remaining egg, a little at a time, into the partly cooled mixture. Continue beating until the dough forms a smooth, shiny paste.

Spoon 12 mounds of the chou-puff dough, spaced well apart, onto the prepared baking sheet. Brush them with the reserved beaten egg and sprinkle them with the sesame seeds. Bake until the dough is crisp and golden brown—20 to 25 minutes. Using the point of a sharp knife, pierce each puff to allow the steam to escape, then return the puffs to the oven for five minutes more to dry out.

Transfer the whole-wheat puffs to a wire rack and allow them to cool.

To make the filling, beat together the ricotta and honey until the mixture is smooth, then gently fold in the raspberries. Split the puffs horizontally and scoop out any soft dough inside. Spoon some filling onto each bottom half, replace the tops, and sift a little confectioners' sugar over them.

Orange and Date Choux

Makes 14 choux
Working time: about 1 hour and 15 minutes
Total time: about 2 hours

Per chou:
Calories **160**
Protein **3g.**
Cholesterol **50mg.**
Total fat **7g.**
Saturated fat **5g.**
Sodium **20mg.**

28 small unblemished rose leaves
3 oz. semisweet chocolate
chou-puff dough (recipe, page 10)
2 tsp. confectioners' sugar
orange slices (optional)
Fruit filling
3 oranges
1½ cups fresh dates, pitted and coarsely chopped, or 1¼ cups pitted dried dates, coarsely chopped
⅛ tsp. ground cinnamon
2 tsp. confectioners' sugar
6 tbsp. plain low-fat yogurt
¼ cup whipping cream

First, prepare the chocolate leaves for decoration. Wash and dry the rose leaves thoroughly. Melt the chocolate on a flameproof plate set over a pan of simmering water, stirring gently. Holding each leaf by its stem, gently press the underside of the leaf into the melted chocolate, then pull it across the side of the plate to remove excess chocolate. Place the leaves, chocolate side up, on a clean plate and allow them to set in a cool place—not the refrigerator.

Preheat the oven to 425° F. Line three baking sheets with parchment paper and draw a total of fourteen 2½-inch circles, spaced well apart, on the parchment; turn the papers over.

Spoon the chou-puff dough into a pastry bag fitted with a ½-inch plain tip. Beginning in the center of each circle, pipe a continuous spiral of chou-puff dough to fill each circle. Bake the puffs until they are well risen, golden brown, and crisp—25 to 30 minutes. Remove the choux from the oven, pierce a hole in the side of each with the tip of a sharp knife, then return them to the oven for another five minutes to dry out the insides. Cool the puffs on wire racks.

To make the filling, grate the zest of 1 orange into a mixing bowl and add the dates. Slice off the zest and pith from all 3 oranges, and cut them into segments (box, opposite). Cut each segment into two or three pieces, and add them to the mixing bowl. Mix the cinnamon and confectioners' sugar into the yogurt, then gently fold this into the date and orange mixture. Whip the cream until it is stiff, and place it in a pastry bag fitted with a ½-inch star tip.

Cut a lid from the top of each puff, and remove any uncooked dough from the inside. Spoon the date and orange filling into the puffs, then replace the lids. Sift the confectioners' sugar over the choux, then pipe a whirl of cream on top of each one.

Starting from the stem end, carefully peel off the rose leaves from their chocolate coating and arrange two chocolate leaves in every cream whirl. Serve the choux with slices of orange, if you like.

Segmenting an Orange

1 *REMOVING THE PEEL. Slice off the peel at both ends of the orange. Stand the fruit on a flat end, and slice downward to remove the zest and pith in vertical strips. This technique of cutting away zest and pith together ensures that every trace of pith is removed.*

2 *CUTTING OUT THE SEGMENTS. Working over a bowl to catch the juice, hold the orange in one hand, and slice between flesh and membrane to remove each segment. The segments will now make a fresh and appealing filling or decoration.*

Pear and Hazelnut Puffs

Makes 36 puffs
Working time: about 1 hour
Total time: about 1 hour and 30 minutes

Per puff:
Calories **75**
Protein **2g.**
Cholesterol **20mg.**
Total fat **5g.**
Saturated fat **2g.**
Sodium **30mg.**

⅓ cup hazelnuts, toasted and peeled (technique, page 29), and finely chopped
chou-puff dough (recipe, page 10)
8 large ripe firm pears
1 tsp. fresh lemon juice
1 tbsp. unsalted butter
2 tbsp. sugar
1½ tbsp. confectioners' sugar

Preheat the oven to 425° F. Line two large baking sheets with parchment paper.

Reserve 1 tablespoon of chopped hazelnuts; stir the remainder into the freshly prepared chou-puff dough. Spoon the dough into a pastry bag fitted with a ¾-inch plain tip. Spacing them well apart, pipe 36 small rounds of dough, about 1½ inches in diameter, onto the prepared sheets. Top them with the reserved hazelnuts, pressing the nuts gently into the dough, then bake until the puffs are crisp and golden brown on both the tops and sides—20 to 25 minutes. Using the point of a sharp knife, pierce each puff to allow the steam to escape, then return them to the oven for five minutes more to dry out thoroughly. Let the puffs cool on a wire rack.

While the puffs are baking, peel, core, and thinly slice the pears. Put the slices into a nonreactive saucepan with the lemon juice and 2 teaspoons of water, and cook over medium heat, stirring occasionally, until the mixture is reduced to a soft purée. Increase the heat and cook until the mixture is nearly dry. Stir in the butter and sugar, and continue to cook over high heat until the mixture begins to brown. Drain off any remaining liquid and set the mixture aside to cool.

Just before serving, slit the puffs in half horizontally and spoon the pear filling into the bottom halves. Replace the tops and sift on the confectioners' sugar.

Caramel-Topped Apple Fingers

Makes 20 fingers
Working time: about 1 hour
Total time: about 1 hour and 30 minutes

Per finger:
Calories **70**
Protein **1g.**
Cholesterol **35mg.**
Total fat **4g.**
Saturated fat **2g.**
Sodium **15mg.**

chou-puff dough (recipe, page 10)
4 sweet apples
1 tsp. Calvados
2 tbsp. sour cream
½ cup sugar

Preheat the oven to 425° F. Line a large baking sheet with parchment paper.

Spoon the chou-puff dough into a pastry bag fitted with a ½-inch plain tip. Pipe twenty 3-inch fingers, spaced well apart, onto the prepared sheet, cutting the dough off with a wet knife when the required length is reached. Bake the fingers until the pastry is well risen and golden brown—25 to 30 minutes. Using the tip of a sharp knife, pierce a few small holes in each finger to allow the steam to escape, then bake for five minutes more to dry them out thoroughly.

Turn the fingers out onto a wire rack to cool.

While the fingers are baking and cooling, prepare the filling. Peel, core, and thinly slice the apples into a heavy-bottomed saucepan with 1 tablespoon of water. Cook the sliced apples over low heat, covered, until the liquid has evaporated and the apples have almost the consistency of applesauce. Allow the apples to cool about 30 minutes, then stir in the Calvados and sour cream.

To make the caramel topping, put the sugar and 2 tablespoons of water into a small, heavy-bottomed saucepan placed over low heat, and allow the sugar to dissolve without stirring. Warm a sugar thermometer in hot water, then place it in the pan. Bring the syrup to a boil and cook it rapidly until it turns a rich brown color—the temperature on the thermometer should be between 320° and 338° F. Brush down any sugar crystals stuck to the sides of the pan with a natural-bristle pastry brush dipped in hot water—a nylon brush will disintegrate in the heat.

Remove the pan from the heat and place it, briefly, in a large pan of cold water to arrest the cooking process; then set it in hot water to keep the caramel fluid. Holding the fingers very carefully, dip them into the hot caramel to coat their tops. Place the coated fingers, caramel side up, on a wire rack set over wax paper, and allow the topping to set—about five minutes. Cut the fingers in half horizontally and spoon in a little of the apple mixture. Serve immediately.

Mango and Ginger Puffs

Makes 24 puffs
Working time: about 45 minutes
Total time: about 1 hour and 20 minutes

Per puff:	
Calories **100**	chou-puff dough (recipe, page 10)
Protein **2g.**	¾ cup whipping cream
Cholesterol **30mg.**	2 ripe mangoes, peeled, pitted, and diced
Total fat **5g.**	1 cup confectioners' sugar, sifted
Saturated fat **3g.**	1 tsp. ground ginger
Sodium **40mg.**	

Preheat the oven to 425° F. Line two large baking sheets with parchment paper.

Spoon the dough into a pastry bag fitted with a ½-inch plain tip. Pipe twenty-four 3-inch rings of dough, spaced well apart, onto the prepared sheet; keep the hole in the center of each ring as small as possible—when baked, the rings will close up and form puffs. Bake the rings until they are well risen and golden brown—25 to 30 minutes. Using the tip of a sharp knife, pierce each puff two or three times to allow steam to escape. Return the puffs to the oven for five minutes more to dry out thoroughly, then cool them on a wire rack.

When the puffs are cool, split them horizontally with a sharp knife and remove any uncooked dough from inside. Whip the cream until it is stiff, then transfer it to a pastry bag fitted with a ¼-inch star tip. Pipe a circle of cream around the edge of the lower half of each puff, spoon diced mango into the center, then replace the top halves of the puffs.

Beat the confectioners' sugar and ginger with 2 teaspoons of water until the mixture is smooth and glossy. Fold a wax-paper or parchment-paper pastry bag (technique, page 13), and fill it with the icing. Snip off the tip of the bag and drizzle a zigzag pattern over the tops of the puffs.

White-Wine Éclairs

Makes 20 éclairs
Working time: about 1 hour
Total time: about 3 hours

Per éclair:
Calories **75**
Protein **1g.**
Cholesterol **15mg.**
Total fat **3g.**
Saturated fat **2g.**
Sodium **30mg.**

1 large orange
1 lemon
1¼ cups white wine
¼ cup sugar
3 tbsp. cornstarch
2 tbsp. whipping cream
7 tbsp. confectioners' sugar
Chou-puff dough
½ cup white wine
3 tbsp. unsalted butter
½ cup unbleached all-purpose flour
1 whole egg
1 egg white

Begin by preparing the filling and decoration. Using a vegetable peeler, pare the zest from the orange and the lemon, cutting long, thin strips from the top to the bottom. Cut one-third of the orange and lemon strips into fine shreds and set them aside. Put the remaining strips into a saucepan with the wine. Bring the wine just to the boiling point, then remove the saucepan from the heat. Cover the pan and allow the mixture to steep for at least 30 minutes.

In the meantime, put 2 tablespoons of the sugar into a small saucepan with 2 tablespoons of cold water. Heat until the sugar dissolves, then bring the mixture to a boil. Add the finely shredded orange and lemon zest, and cook over low heat until the shreds soften—about one minute. Pour the shreds into a fine sieve to drain; discard the sugar syrup. Line a small tray with parchment paper. Separate the shreds and place them individually on the paper, then set them aside to dry.

Using a slotted spoon, remove the strips of orange and lemon zest from the wine, and discard them. In a small bowl, blend the cornstarch with a little of the wine to make a smooth paste. Gradually stir the cornstarch mixture and the remaining sugar into the wine in the saucepan. Bring to a boil over medium heat, stirring constantly until the mixture thickens and clears. Lower the heat and continue stirring for two to three minutes more to ensure that the cornstarch is thoroughly cooked. Remove the saucepan from the heat, and cover the surface of the mixture with plastic wrap to prevent a skin from forming. Set the saucepan aside and allow the wine mixture to cool completely—about 20 minutes.

Whip the cream until it forms soft peaks. When the wine mixture is cool, whisk it until smooth, then grad-

ually fold in the cream. Re-cover the surface of the wine cream with plastic wrap and refrigerate it while you make the éclairs.

Preheat the oven to 425° F. Line one large baking sheet, or two small ones, with parchment paper.

Prepare the chou-puff dough as directed on page 10, using the ingredients listed at left—here, wine replaces the water. Put the chou-puff dough into a pastry bag fitted with a ½-inch star tip. Pipe twenty 3-inch lengths, spaced well apart, onto the lined baking sheet, cutting the dough off with a small knife at the correct length. Bake the éclairs until they are well risen and golden brown—20 to 25 minutes. Pierce each éclair with the tip of a small knife to allow the steam to escape, then return them to the oven for five minutes more to dry out. Transfer the éclairs to a wire rack to cool.

Using a sharp knife, cut each éclair in half horizontally. Pipe or spoon the wine cream into the base of each one, and replace the top.

Sift the confectioners' sugar into a bowl, and blend it with 3 teaspoons of boiling water to make a smooth icing. Using a pastry brush, brush the icing over the top of the éclairs, then decorate them with the orange and lemon shreds. Set the éclairs aside in a cool place until the icing sets—20 to 30 minutes. To ensure that the éclairs are crisp, serve them on the day they are made.

Mini Paris-Brest

THE FIRST PARIS-BREST WAS NAMED BY A TURN-
OF-THE-CENTURY FRENCH PASTRY CHEF IN HONOR OF THE
FAMOUS BICYCLE RACE OF THE SAME NAME. RING-
SHAPED TO RESEMBLE A WHEEL, IT WAS TRADITIONALLY FILLED
WITH AN ALMOND PRALINE PASTRY CREAM. HERE,
THE EGGS ARE OMITTED AND HAZELNUTS—WHICH HAVE LESS
FAT THAN ALMONDS—ARE USED IN THE PRALINE,
MAKING A LIGHTER PASTRY CREAM.

Makes 20 rings
Working time: about 1 hour
Total time: about 2 hours

Per ring:
Calories **100**
Protein **2g.**
Cholesterol **35mg.**
Total fat **7g.**
Saturated fat **4g.**
Sodium **20mg.**

chou-puff dough (recipe, page 10)
3 oz. hazelnuts, toasted and peeled (technique, page 29)
⅓ cup sugar
4 tbsp. whipping cream
1 cup sour cream
1 tbsp. confectioners' sugar
3 candied cherries, thinly sliced (optional)

Preheat the oven to 425° F. Line two baking sheets with parchment paper, then draw a total of 20 circles on the paper, using a 2½-inch plain cutter as a guide. Invert the paper so that the pencil marks face down.

Spoon the chou-puff dough into a pastry bag fitted with a ½-inch star tip. Following the drawn circles, pipe rings of dough onto the parchment paper. Bake them until they are well risen, golden brown, and firm to the touch—20 to 25 minutes. Using the point of a sharp knife, pierce each ring in several places around the outside to allow the steam to escape, then return them to the oven for five minutes to dry out completely. Let them cool on wire racks. As soon as the rings are cool, cut each one in half horizontally and scoop out any uncooked dough. Keep the rings in matching pairs.

Lightly butter a small baking sheet for the praline. Put the hazelnuts and sugar into a small, heavy-bottomed saucepan, and stir over low heat until the sugar dissolves and turns a golden caramel color. Immediately pour the nut mixture onto the buttered sheet. Leave it in a cool place until it has set hard—about 30 minutes.

Break the hardened praline into pieces and put them into a strong plastic bag placed inside another. Crush to a fine powder with a mallet or a wooden rolling pin. Pass the praline through a coarse metal sieve and return any large pieces to the bag for crushing.

Whip the cream until it is stiff. Gently mix in the sour cream, then fold in the hazelnut praline, reserving 1 tablespoon for decoration.

Spoon a little praline cream into the bottom half of each ring, then replace the tops. Sift confectioners' sugar lightly over the rings, and decorate them with cherry slices, if you wish, and a sprinkling of the reserved praline.

Chocolate-Caramel Éclairs

Makes 24 éclairs
Working time: about 50 minutes
Total time: about 1 hour and 50 minutes

Per éclair:
Calories **75**
Protein **1g.**
Cholesterol **30mg.**
Total fat **4g.**
Saturated fat **2g.**
Sodium **10mg.**

chou-puff dough (recipe, page 10)
¾ cup sugar
1 oz. pistachio nuts, peeled and chopped
1¼ cups chocolate-flavored pastry cream (recipe, page 11)

Preheat the oven to 425° F. Line two large baking sheets with parchment paper.

Spoon the chou-puff dough into a pastry bag fitted with a ½-inch plain tip. Pipe twenty-four 3-inch lengths of dough, spaced well apart, onto the prepared baking sheets, cutting the mixture off at the tip with a wet knife at the correct length. Bake until the pastry is well risen, golden brown, and crisp—25 to 30 minutes. Using the point of a sharp knife, pierce a small hole in one end of each éclair. Return the éclairs to the oven for five minutes to dry out completely. Let them cool on wire racks.

To make the caramel, put the sugar into a small, heavy-bottomed saucepan with ⅓ cup of water, and stir over low heat until the sugar has dissolved. Brush down any sugar crystals stuck to the sides of the pan with a natural-bristle pastry brush dipped in hot water—a nylon brush will disintegrate in the heat. Warm a candy thermometer in hot water, then place it in the pan. Boil the syrup rapidly until the temperature on the thermometer registers between 320° and 338° F.; the syrup will have turned a light golden brown. Remove the pan from the heat and place it briefly in a large pan of cold water to arrest the cooking process; then set the pan in hot water to keep the caramel fluid. Holding each éclair carefully with your fingers, dip the top into the caramel. Sprinkle the éclairs immediately with pistachio nuts, and place them on a wire rack set over a sheet of wax paper. Set the éclairs aside until the caramel hardens—about five minutes.

Put the pastry cream into a pastry bag fitted with a ½-inch star tip. Slit each éclair along one side, just under the caramel topping, open them, and fill them with pastry cream.

Serve the éclairs within two to three hours of filling. Until then, keep them in a cool dry place—a damp or humid atmosphere will make the caramel sticky.

EDITOR'S NOTE: *To peel pistachio nuts, blanch them in boiling water for one minute, drain them thoroughly, then rub them vigorously in a towel.*

Phyllo Fans

Makes 16 fans
Working time: about 45 minutes
Total time: about 55 minutes

Per fan:
Calories **80**
Protein **1g.**
Cholesterol **15mg.**
Total fat **3g.**
Saturated fat **1g.**
Sodium **20mg.**

½ cup ground almonds
⅔ cup plus 1 tbsp. light brown sugar
2 lemons, grated zest and juice
1 tbsp. skim milk
1 egg
4 sheets phyllo pastry, each about 18 by 12 inches
1 tsp. safflower oil
1 oz. semisweet chocolate

Place the ground almonds in a mixing bowl with 1 tablespoon of the sugar, the lemon zest, and the skim milk. Add the egg and beat the mixture to form a smooth paste.

In a heavy-bottomed saucepan over low heat, make a lemon glaze by heating the lemon juice with the remaining sugar. Stir until the sugar dissolves, then bring the mixture to a boil and cook it until it is syrupy—about two minutes. Set the glaze aside to cool.

Preheat the oven to 400° F.

Stack the sheets of phyllo and keep them covered with a damp cloth.

Lay one sheet of phyllo on a work surface and spread it evenly with half the almond mixture. Cover this with another sheet of phyllo and press it down lightly. Cut the sheets in half widthwise, then into fourths lengthwise, to form eight filled strips, each 9 by 3 inches.

Starting from the short edge of one strip, fold it into 8 to 10 even pleats. Transfer the pleated strip to a baking sheet, and pinching the pleats together at one end, open out the other end into a fan shape. Repeat this procedure with the other strips, then use the remaining filling and pastry to make eight more fans.

Brush the fans lightly with the oil and bake them until they are deep gold—seven to eight minutes. Remove the fans from the oven and brush them with the lemon glaze. Set them aside to cool.

Break the chocolate into a flameproof bowl set over a pan of hot but not boiling water. Stir gently until the chocolate has melted, then fill a small wax-paper or parchment-paper pastry bag *(technique, page 13)* with the melted chocolate. Cut a small hole at the tip of the bag and decorate the fans with fine piping.

Phyllo-Wrapped Fruit

Makes 12 fruit
Working time: about 30 minutes
Total time: about 1 hour and 20 minutes

Per fruit:
Calories **50**
Protein **1g.**
Cholesterol **10mg.**
Total fat **2g.**
Saturated fat **1g.**
Sodium **15mg.**

4 sheets phyllo pastry, each about 18 by 12 inches
4 very ripe apricots, halved and pitted
4 very ripe plums, halved and pitted
4 figs, peeled and halved
2 tbsp. unsalted butter, melted
1 tsp. sliced almonds
confectioners' sugar, to decorate
Rose-water filling
1¼ cups skim milk
3½ tbsp. enriched farina
1 tsp. sugar
3 tsp. rose water

To make the filling, bring the milk to a boil over medium heat. Sprinkle in the enriched farina and stir continuously until the mixture returns to a boil. Lower the heat and simmer for two minutes, then stir in the sugar and rose water. Set aside to cool.

Meanwhile, cut each sheet of phyllo into six 6-inch squares. Stack the 24 squares and cover them with a damp cloth, removing them as they are needed.

Spread some of the cooled filling onto the cut surfaces of each piece of fruit, filling the cavities in the apricots and plums, then sandwich the fruit halves back together again to form whole fruit.

Preheat the oven to 350° F. Wrap each fruit in two squares of phyllo: To wrap the apricots, place each fruit on its side at the center of one edge of a phyllo square, and roll it up. Twist both ends like a candy wrapper, brush with melted butter, then roll the wrapped fruit in a second square of phyllo in the same way. For the plums, place each fruit, stem end up, in the center of a phyllo square. Gather the pastry up around the fruit and twist it at the top. Brush with melted butter, then wrap the fruit in a second square. Smooth the top edges of pastry down over the fruit. Wrap figs in the same way as plums, but ease open the layers of pastry at the top of the fruit rather than smoothing them flat.

Place the wrapped fruit, spaced well apart, on a lightly buttered baking sheet. Brush a little more melted butter onto each one and sprinkle the almonds over the apricots. Bake until the pastries are lightly browned at the edges—about 18 minutes. Transfer to a wire rack. As soon as the pastries are cool—about 30 minutes—sift a little confectioners' sugar over each one and serve.

EDITOR'S NOTE: *If rose water is unavailable, 3 teaspoons of fresh orange juice or ½ teaspoon of vanilla extract may be substituted.*

Quince and Chestnut Strudel

Makes 18 slices
Working time: about 1 hour
Total time: about 2 hours and 40 minutes

Per slice:
Calories **235**
Protein **7g.**
Cholesterol **15mg.**
Total fat **6g.**
Saturated fat **4g.**
Sodium **190mg.**

1 lb. fresh quinces
½ cup light brown sugar
½ lemon, grated zest and juice
1 stick cinnamon
4 oz. chestnuts
8 oz. low-fat cream cheese
1 tsp. ground cinnamon
1 tsp. finely grated orange zest
3 sheets phyllo pastry, each about 18 by 12 inches
2 tbsp. unsalted butter, melted
1 tbsp. confectioners' sugar

Peel and core the quinces, and cut them lengthwise into ¾-inch-thick slices, reserving the skins. Place the slices in acidulated water to prevent discoloration. In a nonreactive saucepan, dissolve the brown sugar in 1¼ cups of water. Add the lemon zest and juice, the cinnamon stick, and the quince skins, and simmer for about 20 minutes. Strain the syrup and return it to the pan. Drain the quince slices and poach them in the syrup until they are tender—about 30 minutes.

Meanwhile, peel the chestnuts *(box, below),* simmer them in a saucepan of water until they are tender but unbroken—about 20 minutes—then drain and coarsely chop them.

Using a slotted spoon, transfer the poached quince slices to a plate to cool. Reserve 2 tablespoons of the poaching syrup. In a mixing bowl, combine the cheese, reserved syrup, ground cinnamon, and orange zest.

Preheat the oven to 375° F., and lightly grease a baking sheet.

Place a sheet of phyllo on a work surface, keeping the others covered with a damp cloth, and brush the sheet lightly with a little of the melted butter. Fold it in half widthwise to form a 12-by-9-inch rectangle. Spread one-third of the cheese mixture down one long side of the phyllo sheet, leaving a 1½-inch margin free of filling along the edge and at each end. Arrange one-third of the chestnuts on top of the cheese mixture and one-third of the quince slices on top of the chestnuts. Roll the long edge of the pastry over so as just to enclose the filling. Brush the other three edges of the pastry with more melted butter. Fold the two short edges over the filling and roll up the pastry lengthwise. Place the strudel, seam downward, on the prepared baking sheet, and brush the top with a little more melted butter. Assemble and roll up two more strudels in the same way.

Bake the strudels until they are crisp and golden brown—35 to 45 minutes. Cool them on a wire rack, and dust them with a little sifted confectioners' sugar just before you slice and serve them.

EDITOR'S NOTE: *Firm pears may replace the quinces: They should be poached for 10 minutes only and drained on paper towels; 2 tablespoons of gooseberry or other tart preserves should be added to the cheese mixture. The unbaked strudels may be frozen and baked when they are needed.*

Peeling Chestnuts

1 PREPARING THE CHESTNUTS. With a sharp knife, cut a cross in the hull of each chestnut. Drop the chestnuts into boiling water and parboil them for about 10 minutes to loosen their hulls. Remove the saucepan from the heat.

2 PEELING OFF THE SKINS. With a slotted spoon, lift out the chestnuts a few at a time. Peel off the hulls and inner skins while the chestnuts are hot.

Muesli and Apple Strudel

Makes 12 slices
Working time: about 30 minutes
Total time: about 1 hour and 30 minutes

Per slice:
Calories **60**
Protein **1g.**
Cholesterol **trace**
Total fat **2g.**
Saturated fat **1g.**
Sodium **20mg.**

2 tsp. safflower oil
½ cup sugar-free muesli with high fruit and nut content
2 tbsp. light brown sugar
.1 tsp. ground cinnamon
4 sheets phyllo pastry, each about 18 by 12 inches
1 tbsp. unsalted butter, melted
12 oz. cooking apples, peeled, cored, and thinly sliced
1 tsp. confectioners' sugar

Preheat the oven to 400° F.

To make the filling, heat the oil in a small saucepan.

Add the muesli and cook it over medium-low heat until crisp—about two minutes. Stir in the light brown sugar and ½ teaspoon of the cinnamon, and set the mixture aside to cool.

Place a sheet of phyllo on a work surface and brush it lightly with melted butter. Lay the remaining sheets over the first, brushing each one with a little melted butter. Arrange the apple slices evenly along one long edge of the phyllo, and sprinkle them with the muesli mixture. Starting from the long filled edge, roll up the phyllo, enclosing the filling, and place it, seam down, on a lightly buttered baking sheet. (Bend the strudel into a crescent if the baking sheet is too small.)

Brush the strudel with the remaining melted butter, and bake it until the pastry is crisp and golden—about 30 minutes. Cool on a wire rack or serve hot, straight from the oven. Before serving, combine the confectioners' sugar and remaining cinnamon, and sift over the top of the strudel. Cut diagonally into 12 slices.

Almond Spirals

Makes 18 spirals
Working time: about 35 minutes
Total time: about 50 minutes

Per spiral:
Calories **85**
Protein **2g.**
Cholesterol **trace**
Total fat **6g.**
Saturated fat **2g.**
Sodium **5mg.**

1 cup ground almonds
7 tbsp. sugar
1 egg white
¼ tsp. pure almond extract
6 sheets phyllo pastry, each about 18 by 12 inches
3 tbsp. unsalted butter, melted
confectioners' sugar to decorate

In a mixing bowl, combine the ground almonds, sugar, egg white, and almond extract to form a smooth paste. Divide the paste into 18 equal portions.

Cut each sheet of phyllo widthwise into three 12-by-6-inch rectangles. Stack all 18 rectangles in one pile, then cover them with a clean, damp cloth.

Preheat the oven to 375° F.

Assemble the spirals one at a time to prevent the phyllo from drying out. Take a portion of almond paste, and roll it on a work surface into an 11½-inch long, thin sausage shape. If the paste sticks, powder the work surface with a little confectioners' sugar. Place a sheet of phyllo on the work top and brush with a little melted butter, then place the roll of almond paste along one long edge of the pastry. Roll up the phyllo, enclosing the almond filling, then shape the roll into a spiral. Repeat this process until all the portions of almond paste and phyllo rectangles have been made into spirals.

Arrange the spirals on baking trays, pressing the loose ends against the sides of the trays to prevent them from unrolling. Brush each spiral with melted butter, then bake them until they are golden brown—12 to 15 minutes.

Remove the spirals from the oven and cool them on wire racks. Before serving, sift a little confectioners' sugar over each pastry to decorate it.

Poppy-Seed Pillows

Makes 16 pillows
Working time: about 35 minutes
Total time: about 1 hour

Per pillow:
Calories **110**
Protein **3g.**
Cholesterol **trace**
Total fat **6g.**
Saturated fat **1g.**
Sodium **25mg.**

⅔ cup plus 1 tsp. poppy seeds
1 cup fresh orange juice
¾ cup golden raisins
¼ cup light brown sugar
1 orange, grated zest only
⅛ tsp. pumpkin pie spice
6 sheets phyllo pastry, each about 18 by 12 inches
2 tbsp. unsalted butter, melted

Finely grind ⅔ cup of the poppy seeds in a coffee grinder and place them in a saucepan with the orange juice. (Alternatively, blend the seeds and juice in a food processor or a blender.) Stir in the golden raisins, sugar, orange zest, and pumpkin pie spice, and bring the mixture to a boil. Lower the heat and simmer gently until the mixture is pulpy—about 15 minutes. Let it cool. Meanwhile, preheat the oven to 400° F.

Keep the sheets of phyllo covered with a damp cloth to prevent them from drying out. Remove one sheet, lay it on a work surface, and brush it with melted butter. Cover it with a second sheet of phyllo, brush on more melted butter, then lay a third sheet on top. Cut the layered sheets lengthwise into two equal strips, then cut each strip widthwise into fourths, to give a total of eight 6-by-4½-inch rectangles.

Divide half of the poppy-seed mixture among the eight rectangles: Spoon the mixture along one long edge, leaving a 1-inch margin free of filling along the edge and at each end. Fold the long edge over to enclose the filling, and fold in the two shorter side edges, pressing them down gently; continue rolling up the pastry lengthwise to make a pillow-shaped parcel. Place the parcel on a baking sheet, seam side down, and fold the remaining phyllo rectangles in the same way. Use the remaining phyllo sheets and poppy-seed mixture to make another eight pillows.

Brush the pillows with a little more melted butter and sprinkle them with the reserved teaspoon of poppy seeds. Bake until the pastries are crisp and golden—seven to eight minutes. Serve warm or cold.

Tangerine Cream Pastries

Makes 6 pastries
Working time: about 40 minutes
Total time: about 1 hour

Per pastry:
Calories **105**
Protein **2g.**
Cholesterol **20mg.**
Total fat **4g.**
Saturated fat **1g.**
Sodium **15mg.**

4 tangerines
5 tbsp. sugar
2 sheets phyllo pastry, each about 18 by 12 inches
1 tbsp. safflower oil
⅓ cup orange-flavored pastry cream (recipe, page 11)

Preheat the oven to 425° F.

Using a potato peeler, pare the zest of two of the tangerines, taking care not to include any of the white pith. Cut the zest into fine shreds. Put the sugar into a saucepan with ½ cup of water and heat on low, stirring, until the sugar dissolves; then bring it to a boil without stirring. Add the strips of zest to the syrup and simmer them gently for about 20 minutes. Remove the strips with a slotted spoon and let them drain in a sieve set over a bowl.

Meanwhile, lightly oil two baking sheets. Lay the sheets of phyllo on a work surface. Using a 3½-inch plain cutter, cut 12 circles from each sheet. Brush the circles very lightly with oil, then stack them, oiled side up, in pairs on the baking sheets. Bake them until they are crisp and golden—four to five minutes. Carefully transfer the 12 paired circles to a wire rack to cool.

Peel the tangerines—including those without the zest—and carefully remove all the pith. Divide them into segments, removing the seeds and as much of the membrane as possible. Take six of the paired pastry circles, and arrange five or six tangerine segments on each one. Spoon 1 tablespoon of pastry cream over the fruit, then place the remaining pairs of pastry circles on top. Decorate the pastries with the candied tangerine zest and serve immediately.

Cherry Cheese Tartlets

Makes 12 tartlets
Working time: about 45 minutes
Total time: about 1 hour and 10 minutes

Per tartlet:
Calories **100**
Protein **5g.**
Cholesterol **20mg.**
Total fat **3g.**
Saturated fat **1g.**
Sodium **110mg.**

| 3 sheets phyllo pastry, each about 18 by 12 inches |
| 1 tbsp. unsalted butter, melted |
| **Spicy cheese filling** |
| 8 oz. low-fat cream cheese, softened |
| ½ cup plain low-fat yogurt |
| 1 egg |
| 1 tbsp. honey |
| 1 tsp. pure vanilla extract |
| ½ tsp. ground cinnamon |
| **Glossy cherry topping** |
| 1 tbsp. cherry jam |
| ½ tsp. cornstarch |
| 12 oz. sweet cherries, pitted and halved |

Preheat the oven to 375° F.

Trim 2 inches off one of the short edges of each sheet of phyllo, then cut each sheet into twelve 4-inch squares. Keep the squares covered with a damp cloth to prevent them from drying out, removing them as needed. Brush twelve 3-inch round tart pans with a little of the melted butter. Stack three squares of phyllo pastry in each pan, fold the edges over to neaten them, then brush the tops lightly with melted butter. Bake the cases in the oven until they are crisp and lightly browned—about three minutes. Allow the cases to cool in the pans.

In the meantime, prepare the cheese filling. Put the cheese, yogurt, egg, honey, vanilla extract, and cinnamon into a mixing bowl. Beat the ingredients together with a wooden spoon until smooth, or blend the mixture in a food processor. Divide the filling equally among the pastry cases, spreading it evenly with the back of a teaspoon. Return the tartlets to the oven and cook them until the filling has set—8 to 10 minutes. Remove the tartlets from the oven and cool them in the pans.

While the tartlets are cooling, prepare the cherry topping. First, make a glaze by stirring the cherry jam with 3 tablespoons of water in a small saucepan set over low heat. Blend the cornstarch to a smooth paste with 1 tablespoon of water. Add the cornstarch paste to the jam solution, bring the mixture to a boil, and cook, stirring, until it thickens and becomes translucent—about two minutes. Arrange the cherry halves on top of the cheese mixture, and brush them with the cherry glaze.

Allow the glaze to set for a few minutes before unmolding and serving the tartlets.

Cherry Triangles

Makes 12 triangles
Working time: about 40 minutes
Total time: about 1 hour and 20 minutes

Per triangle:	6 tbsp. plain low-fat yogurt
Calories **90**	1 tbsp. sugar
Protein **2g.**	1 tbsp. kirsch
Cholesterol **0mg.**	1 lb. sweet cherries, pitted
Total fat **6g.**	8 sheets phyllo pastry, each about 18 by 12 inches
Saturated fat **trace**	3 tsp. safflower oil
Sodium **25mg.**	confectioners' sugar to decorate

First, make the filling. Place the yogurt, sugar, and kirsch in a mixing bowl. Reserve 12 cherries for decoration. Quarter the remainder and gently fold them into the yogurt mixture.

Preheat the oven to 400° F. Keep the sheets of phyllo covered with a damp cloth to prevent them from drying out, removing them as needed.

Lay one sheet of phyllo on a work surface. Brush it lightly with oil and cover it with a second sheet. Cut this double sheet of phyllo lengthwise into three strips, each 4 inches wide. Place one tablespoon of filling at one end of a strip, then fold a corner of the phyllo over the filling to form a neat triangle. Continue folding the filled triangle until you reach the end of the strip, keeping the shape as you work. Tuck in the loose end of the phyllo and transfer the triangular parcel—seam side down—to a lightly oiled baking sheet. Make up the two remaining strips in the same way, then repeat the process with the rest of the phyllo and filling to make nine more triangles.

Brush the phyllo triangles with the remaining oil, and bake them until they are crisp and golden—9 to 10 minutes. Transfer them to a wire rack to cool.

Before serving, halve the reserved cherries. Sift a little confectioners' sugar over the top of each triangle and serve with the cherries.

Fruited Phyllo Cigars

Makes 24 cigars
Working time: about 25 minutes
Total time: about 9 hours and 45 minutes
(includes soaking and cooling)

Per cigar:
Calories **35**
Protein **trace**
Cholesterol **0mg.**
Total fat **2g.**
Saturated fat **0g.**
Sodium **15mg.**

¾ cup mixed dried fruit (peaches, pears, apple rings, apricots), finely chopped
2 tsp. ground coriander
1½ tbsp. safflower oil
2 sheets phyllo pastry, each about 18 by 12 inches
2 tbsp. confectioners' sugar

Put the mixed dried fruit into a small, nonreactive saucepan, pour about ¾ cup of boiling water over it, cover the pan, and let the fruit soak for at least eight hours, or overnight.

When the fruit is plump, place the pan over low heat and simmer the fruit, uncovered, until it is soft and the water has evaporated. Remove the pan from the heat, stir in the coriander, and let the fruit cool.

Preheat the oven to 350° F.

Lightly oil a large baking sheet. Lay one sheet of phyllo on top of the other. Cut the sheets lengthwise into four equal strips, then cut each strip widthwise into three, to give a total of twenty-four 6-by-3-inch rectangles. Stack them together in one pile. Brush the top rectangle with a little oil, and place a teaspoonful of the cooled fruit mixture along one of its shorter edges, leaving ½ inch free of filling at each end. Roll up the phyllo around the fruit to form a cigar shape, then place the cigar, seam side down, on the baking sheet. Brush the next rectangle with oil and repeat the process, continuing until all the filling and phyllo rectangles have been used.

Bake the phyllo cigars until they are crisp and golden—15 to 20 minutes. Transfer them to a wire rack to cool, and sift the confectioners' sugar over them before serving.

Chocolate and Fruit Phyllo Flowers

Makes 4 flowers
Working time: about 35 minutes
Total time: about 50 minutes

Per flower:	
Calories **155**	4 sheets phyllo pastry, each about 18 by 12 inches
Protein **4g.**	
Cholesterol **10mg.**	1 tbsp. unsalted butter, melted
Total fat **9g.**	1½ oz. semisweet chocolate
Saturated fat **4g.**	6 tbsp. plain low-fat yogurt
Sodium **35mg.**	4 strawberries, hulled and sliced
	10 seedless green grapes, halved

Preheat the oven to 375° F. Cut each sheet of phyllo in half lengthwise, then in quarters widthwise, to yield thirty-two 6-by-4½-inch rectangles. Keep the phyllo rectangles covered with a damp cloth to prevent them from drying out, removing them as they are needed.

Brush four 4-inch shallow tart pans with a little melted butter. Line one pan with four pieces of phyllo arranged at different angles, brush lightly with melted butter, then arrange another four pieces of phyllo on top at different angles from the first batch. Line each pan with pastry in the same way, then brush the top layer lightly with melted butter.

Bake the phyllo cases in the oven until they are crisp and golden brown—six to eight minutes. Allow the cases to cool in the pans.

Melt the chocolate in a flameproof bowl set over a pan of hot but not boiling water. Using a fine-bristled brush, spread half of the melted chocolate inside the phyllo cases.

Place the yogurt in a bowl and blend in the remaining chocolate. Divide the yogurt mixture among the phyllo flower cases, and arrange the strawberry slices and grape halves to resemble petals. Carefully unmold the flowers and serve immediately.

Kataifi Nests with Orange Custard

KATAIFI IS A GREEK PASTRY MADE IN LONG, THIN STRANDS. IT CAN BE BOUGHT ALREADY PREPARED FROM MIDDLE EASTERN SPECIALTY SHOPS; IF *KATAIFI* IS UNAVAILABLE, SUBSTITUTE PHYLLO, CUT AND SHAPED AS DESCRIBED FOR THE ALMOND AND PERSIMMON STARS ON PAGE 62.

Makes 16 nests
Working time: about 1 hour
Total time: about 2 hours (includes soaking)

Per nest:
Calories **70**
Protein **3g.**
Cholesterol **20mg.**
Total fat **2g.**
Saturated fat **1g.**
Sodium **15mg.**

½ lb. kataifi pastry, at room temperature
1½ tbsp. unsalted butter, melted
⅓ cup dried apricots, ¼ cup soaked in water for 30 minutes, soaking water reserved, remaining apricots diced
1 stick cinnamon
1-inch strip lemon zest
2 tbsp. fresh lemon juice
1 tbsp. honey
3 tbsp. sour cream
½ tsp. ground cinnamon
Orange custard
2 tsp. cornstarch
½ cup skim milk
1 egg yolk
2 tsp. honey
1 tsp. pure vanilla extract
1 tsp. orange-flower water or fresh orange juice
½ tsp. finely grated orange zest
1 tbsp. powdered gelatin

Preheat the oven to 375° F.

Knead the *kataifi* pastry, while it is still in the packet, to soften the strands and ease separation. Remove the required quantity from the packet and ease out the strands a little more with your hands. Divide the *kataifi* into 16 equal portions. Press one portion into a 2-inch muffin pan, forming a small nest of pastry by pressing down in the center and up the sides of the pan. Brush the nest with a little of the melted butter. Form the other 15 nests in the same way, then bake them until they are golden brown—about 20 minutes. Turn them out to cool on a wire rack.

While the nests are baking, put the soaked apricots and their soaking water into a saucepan, and add the cinnamon stick, lemon zest and juice, and honey. Bring the water to a boil, then lower the heat and simmer the mixture until the apricots are tender—about 20 minutes—adding more water as necessary. Using a slotted spoon, transfer the apricots to a plate and let them cool. Strain the liquid, then return it to the pan and boil it down until only 4 tablespoons remain; reserve this syrup for glazing the pastries.

To make the custard, mix the cornstarch and 1 tablespoon of the skim milk until smooth. Beat the egg yolk with the honey, then blend in the cornstarch. Scald the remaining milk, then whisk it into the egg mixture. Return the custard to the pan and simmer it gently until it has thickened, stirring all the time. Strain the custard through a fine sieve, then beat in the vanilla extract, the orange-flower water or orange juice, and the orange zest. Sprinkle the gelatin over 2 tablespoons of water in a small bowl and allow it to stand for two minutes. Place the bowl over a pan of simmering water and stir until the gelatin has dissolved. Add the gelatin to the custard, whisking vigorously. Set it aside to cool, covering the surface closely with plastic wrap to prevent a skin from forming.

Finely dice the cooked apricots. Whisk the cooled custard, then fold in the cooked apricots and the sour cream. Spoon a little of this filling into the hollow of each *kataifi* nest. Using a pastry brush, sprinkle a little of the reserved syrup around the edges of each nest, and decorate the filling with a piece of diced dried apricot and a sprinkling of ground cinnamon. Serve at room temperature or chilled.

Pumpkin and Pistachio Pastries

Makes 6 pastries
Working time: about 45 minutes
Total time: about 1 hour and 45 minutes

Per pastry:
Calories **175**
Protein **4g.**
Cholesterol **20mg.**
Total fat **10g.**
Saturated fat **3g.**
Sodium **135mg.**

1-lb. slice of fresh pumpkin or butternut squash
⅓ cup pistachio nuts
3 tbsp. honey
2 tbsp. fresh lemon juice
1 tsp. ground cinnamon
½ tsp. grated nutmeg
⅔ cup sour cream
1 egg white
¼ tsp. salt
6 sheets phyllo pastry, each about 18 by 12 inches
2 tbsp. unsalted butter, melted
1 tbsp. light brown sugar
2 tsp. confectioners' sugar

Place the pumpkin or squash slice, skin side down, in a steamer set over a saucepan of lightly boiling water, and steam until tender—20 to 30 minutes. Meanwhile, blanch the pistachio nuts in boiling water for one minute, drain them thoroughly, then rub them vigorously in a towel to remove their skins. Coarsely chop the nuts.

Peel the pumpkin or squash slice, chop the flesh coarsely, and purée it in a blender with the honey, lemon juice, cinnamon, and nutmeg. Transfer the purée to a mixing bowl. Reserve 1 tablespoon of sour cream for decoration, and stir the remainder into the purée, mixing well. In a separate bowl, beat the egg white with the salt until it forms soft peaks. Fold it gently but thoroughly into the purée and put the mixture in the refrigerator to chill.

Preheat the oven to 350° F.

Lay one sheet of phyllo pastry on a work surface, keeping the others covered with a damp cloth to prevent them from drying out. Fold the sheet in half widthwise to make a 12-by-9-inch rectangle. Brush it lightly with a little of the melted butter. Sprinkle one-sixth of the pistachio nuts along one long edge of the pastry rectangle, leaving 1 inch free of nuts at each end. Sprinkle the nuts with a little of the brown sugar.

Fold the long edge of pastry over to enclose the nuts, then fold in ½ inch of pastry along the length of each short side, and press down to seal. Roll up the nut filling until only a 1½-inch strip of phyllo remains unrolled. Shape the pastry into a ring, with the un-rolled strip of phyllo inside, so that the nut-filled roll forms a rim. Overlap the ends of the rim, brush the inside facing edges with melted butter, and press them together to ensure a good seal. To form the base of the case, lift the pastry off the work surface, and neatly pleat and flatten the unrolled phyllo toward the center. Brush the folds with butter, place the case on a flat surface again, and press all the folds and seals firmly together. Repeat this process with the other five sheets of phyllo pastry.

Place the pastry cases on a lightly greased baking sheet, and bake them until they are crisp and deep golden brown—about 20 minutes. Turn them out carefully onto a wire rack to cool.

Shortly before serving, sift a little confectioners' sugar over each pastry rim, and spoon the pumpkin or squash purée into the pastry cases. Stir the reserved sour cream, and swirl a little in the center of each pastry before serving.

Almond and Persimmon Stars

Makes 12 stars
Working time: about 30 minutes
Total time: about 1 hour and 10 minutes

Per star:
Calories **60**
Protein **1g.**
Cholesterol **0mg.**
Total fat **5g.**
Saturated fat **1g.**
Sodium **35mg.**

1 sheet phyllo pastry, about 18 by 12 inches
2 tbsp. polyunsaturated margarine, melted
2 persimmons, peeled, 1 chopped, 1 sliced
3 tbsp. ground almonds
2 tbsp. ground amaretti cookies
1 egg white

Grease and lightly flour twelve 3-inch shallow, flat-bottomed tartlet pans.

Preheat the oven to 400° F.

Spread the phyllo out on a work surface and brush it with the melted margarine. Cut the sheet into twenty-four 3-inch squares. Line each tartlet pan with two squares of phyllo, arranging the corners to form an eight-pointed star.

To make the filling, purée the chopped persimmon in a blender or a food processor. Transfer the purée to a mixing bowl, and stir in the ground almonds and amaretti. In a separate bowl, beat the egg white until it is stiff, then fold it gently into the persimmon-amaretti mixture.

Distribute the filling among the phyllo stars and bake them until the pastry is golden—15 to 20 minutes. Allow the stars to cool briefly in their pans, then unmold them onto wire racks to cool completely.

Decorate each star with the persimmon slices. Serve the stars on the day they are baked, while the pastry is still crisp.

EDITOR'S NOTE: *If amaretti cookies are unobtainable, almond-flavored macaroon crumbs, or any other sweet cookie crumbs, may be substituted.*

Phyllo Fruit Squares

Makes 10 squares
Working time: about 30 minutes
Total time: about 1 hour and 25 minutes

Per square:
Calories **135**
Protein **6g.**
Cholesterol **trace**
Total fat **3g.**
Saturated fat **2g.**
Sodium **25mg.**

2 tbsp. unsalted butter, melted
1 large orange, zest grated, peel and pith removed, flesh cut into segments (technique, page 41)
⅔ cup raisins
⅔ cup golden raisins
1 large cooking apple, peeled and grated
10 sheets phyllo pastry, each about 18 by 12 inches
3 tsp. honey
1 tbsp. sliced almonds
1 tbsp. sugar
2 tsp. fresh orange juice

Preheat the oven to 375° F. Brush an 11-by-7-by-1½-inch baking pan with a little of the melted butter.

Chop the orange segments, and add them to a bowl with both kinds of raisins, the apple, and 2 teaspoons of the orange zest. Mix the fruit together well.

Keep the sheets of phyllo covered with a damp cloth to prevent them from drying out, removing them as they are needed. Lay one sheet of phyllo pastry in the prepared pan so that it overhangs all four sides of the pan. Brush it sparingly with melted butter and cover it with another sheet of phyllo. Brush this with butter and cover it with a third sheet. Sprinkle one-third of the fruit mixture over the phyllo in the pan, and drizzle 1 teaspoon of the honey over the fruit. Fold the four overhanging edges over the filling, one after another, and brush these folded edges with butter.

Repeat the process to make two more layers of phyllo and filling. Lay the final sheet of phyllo over the top, neatly folding the four edges underneath. Brush the top with butter and lightly mark it into a lattice design with a knife. Sprinkle the almonds on top.

Bake until golden brown—25 to 30 minutes. Toward the end of the baking time, prepare a syrup. Heat the sugar and orange juice in a small saucepan with 2 tablespoons of water. Stir the mixture gently until the sugar has dissolved, then boil it for one minute.

Remove the baked phyllo fruit pastry from the oven and pour the syrup over the top. Allow the pastry to cool before you cut it into squares and serve it.

2 *Hazelnut meringue piped into rows of shells awaits the long, gentle cooking that will dry and crisp it (recipe, page 87).*

Light and Airy Creations

Feathery sponge cakes, ethereal meringues, and yeast-leavened cakes all have one essential ingredient in common: air. It is air that gives these pastries their lightness and sublime texture.

Sponge cake, containing the minimum amount of butter *(page 11)*, is the foundation for many of the assemblies on pages 66 to 80. Air trapped within eggs as they are beaten with sugar expands and causes the flour-and-butter mixture to rise during baking. To retain as much air as possible when adding the flour and butter, gently fold them into the eggs with a large spatula, rather than stirring them in. The melted butter must be as cool as possible, or else its warmth will tend to break down air bubbles. Bake the mixture immediately, since it will deflate if left to stand. Any sponge trimmings need not be wasted; use them to make such delicacies as apricot and hazelnut petits fours *(page 113)* and chocolate-dipped stuffed prunes *(page 126)*.

Meringues are nothing more than a magical blend of egg whites, sugar, and air. When beaten vigorously, the egg whites trap air in myriad bubbles. The addition of sugar reinforces the structure of the mixture and makes it firm enough to pipe out. Before the sugar is added, the whites should be beaten until they hold a peak. Add the sugar in small batches, beating well between each addition to return the mixture to a stiff peak. Egg whites and sugar beaten over hot water produce a denser-textured meringue particularly suitable for piping into nests and other containers, as in the fruit-filled meringue baskets on page 91.

Whatever the method of preparation, meringue requires long, slow cooking in the oven to preserve the snow-white color and produce the desired crispness. Some ovens can be a little too hot even at the recommended setting. If in doubt, set your oven to the lowest heat and adjust the cooking time, if necessary. The meringues are ready when they can be lifted easily from the baking paper.

Yeast cakes, rich in B vitamins, are naturally self-rising. Yeast is a living organism that gives off carbon dioxide when it is mixed with a liquid, flour, and sugar. Trapped within the gluten structure of the dough by kneading, the gas gradually expands the mixture, increasing its volume threefold. Warmth accelerates the process, but the yeast will be killed if overheated; normal warm kitchen temperatures are ideal. When a firmer dough is required, as it is for the brioche peaches on page 94 and the Danish pastries on page 98, it must be allowed to rise slowly by being placed in a refrigerator for up to five hours.

Pineapple Sponge Sandwiches

Makes 12 sandwiches
Working time: about 55 minutes
Total time: about 1 hour and 30 minutes

Per sandwich:
Calories **60**
Protein **11g.**
Cholesterol **25mg.**
Total fat **2g.**
Saturated fat **1g.**
Sodium **10mg.**

10 oz. finely chopped fresh pineapple
confectioners' sugar to decorate
Sponge cake
2 cardamom pods, seeds only
1 egg
1 egg white
3 tbsp. sugar
½ cup unbleached all-purpose flour
1 tbsp. unsalted butter, melted and cooled

Preheat the oven to 350° F. Line two large baking sheets with parchment paper.

To make the sponge cake, toast the cardamom seeds in a dry, heavy-bottomed nonstick pan, then crush them very finely. Following the method on page 11, prepare the cake with the ingredients listed above, adding the crushed cardamom seeds to the flour. Using a rubber spatula, spread out the batter in twelve 2½-inch circles on the baking sheets, making sure that the edges are no thinner than the centers. Bake until the circles are lightly colored and set—about six minutes—the edges should not become brown. Immediately after the sponge circles are removed from the oven, transfer them to a wire rack to cool.

Divide the chopped pineapple into 12 equal portions. Just before serving, place a portion of pineapple on half of each sponge circle and carefully fold over the other half. Sift confectioners' sugar over the top. Heat a long metal skewer over a flame or an electric burner, protecting your hand with an oven mitt. When the skewer is red hot, brand a crisscross pattern on the sponge cakes by laying the skewer briefly on the confectioners' sugar, reheating the skewer if necessary.

Layered Fruit Sponge Cakes

Makes 8 sponge cakes
Working time: about 1 hour
Total time: about 1 hour and 10 minutes

Per sponge cake:
Calories **200**
Protein **7g.**
Cholesterol **115mg.**
Total fat **6g.**
Saturated fat **2g.**
Sodium **35mg.**

2 eggs
1 egg white
7 tbsp. sugar
¾ cup unbleached all-purpose flour
1 tbsp. cocoa powder
1 tbsp. confectioners' sugar
Fruit and almond filling
½ lb. cherries, 8 reserved whole for decoration, remainder pitted and chopped
2 nectarines, blanched in boiling water for 30 seconds, peeled, pitted, and chopped
1¼ cups pastry cream (recipe, page 11), made with ½ tsp. pure almond extract instead of 1 tsp. vanilla

Preheat the oven to 350° F.

Line three baking sheets with parchment paper. Draw eight 3-inch circles in pencil, spaced evenly apart,

on each sheet of paper; invert the paper so that the marks face downward.

Put the eggs, egg white, and sugar into a mixing bowl. Place the bowl over a saucepan of hot but not boiling water over low heat. Beat the eggs and sugar together with an electric hand-held mixer until the mixture is thick and very pale. Remove the bowl from the saucepan, and continue beating until the mixture is cool and falls from the whisk in a ribbon. Pour half of the mixture into another bowl. Sift 7 tablespoons of the flour over the surface of the ingredients in one bowl, then fold it in very gently using a large rubber spatula. Fold the remaining flour and the cocoa powder into the ingredients in the other bowl.

Transfer the mixtures into separate nylon pastry bags, each fitted with a ¼-inch plain tip. Pipe 12 rings with the cocoa-flavored mixture, following the outlines drawn on the parchment paper, and pipe a choc-olate dot in the center of each one. Fill in the center rings with the plain mixture. Outline the remaining 12 circles with the plain mixture, pipe a plain dot in the center, and fill the center rings with chocolate mixture.

Bake until the sponge rounds feel firm and are lightly browned—about five minutes. Cool them on the paper for two minutes, then transfer them to a wire rack with a metal spatula and let them cool fully.

Mix together the chopped cherries and nectarines, then assemble the sponge cakes. Spread a little pastry cream over a sponge round and sprinkle it with chopped mixed fruit. Place another sponge layer on top, cover it with pastry cream and fruit, and top with a third sponge round. Make up seven more layered sponge cakes in the same way.

Sift a little confectioners' sugar over the tops of the sponge cakes and place a whole cherry in the center. Serve within an hour of assembling.

Cornets Filled with Fruit Cream

Makes 30 cornets
Working time: about 50 minutes
Total time: about 1 hour and 20 minutes

Per cornet:
Calories **50**
Protein **1g.**
Cholesterol **15mg.**
Total fat **2g.**
Saturated fat **1g.**
Sodium **15mg.**

2 egg whites
¼ cup sugar
½ cup unbleached all-purpose flour
4 tbsp. unsalted butter, melted and cooled
¼ cup mixed candied peel, finely chopped
1¼ cups pastry cream (recipe, page 11)

Preheat the oven to 375° F. Line two large baking sheets with parchment paper.

To make the cornets, first beat the egg whites in a mixing bowl until they are frothy. Sprinkle the sugar over the surface, and beat until the mixture is thick and shiny—two to three minutes. Sift the flour over the surface, then fold it in very gently with the melted butter. Drop 2 to 3 teaspoonfuls of the mixture, spaced well apart, onto one of the baking sheets. Spread each spoonful with the back of a spoon to form a circle 2½ to 3 inches in diameter. Bake until the edges are a light golden brown—about five minutes. Meanwhile, make 2 or 3 more circles on the second baking sheet.

Remove the baked circles from the oven and insert the second baking sheet. Quickly but carefully remove each of the baked circles in turn with a metal spatula, and mold it around a metal cream-horn mold until it is set in shape. If the circles start to harden before they are all shaped, return them to the oven for a minute or so to soften them. Transfer the cornets to a wire rack to cool completely. Bake and shape the remaining mixture in the same way.

Just before serving, fold three-quarters of the mixed candied peel into the pastry cream and spoon it into the cornets. Decorate the filling with the remaining peel and serve.

Filigree Lime Baskets

Makes 8 baskets
Working time: about 40 minutes
Total time: about 1 hour

Per basket:	
Calories **170**	2 egg whites
Protein **3g.**	5 tbsp. confectioners' sugar, sifted
Cholesterol **65mg.**	6 tbsp. cornstarch, sifted
Total fat **5g.**	5 tbsp. unbleached all-purpose flour, sifted
Saturated fat **2g.**	2 tbsp. unsalted butter, melted and cooled
Sodium **35mg.**	½ tsp. pure vanilla extract
	Whipped lime filling
	2 limes
	2 egg yolks
	6 tbsp. sugar
	2 tsp. powdered gelatin
	3 egg whites
	2 tbsp. plain low-fat yogurt
	1¼ cups strawberries, hulled and sliced

Preheat the oven to 425° F. Line a baking sheet with parchment paper. Draw four 4-inch circles on the paper, then invert it so that the markings face downward.

Beat the egg whites in a clean, grease-free bowl until they are white and frothy. Add the sugar and whip until the mixture is well blended, then beat in the cornstarch and flour. Pour in the melted butter and vanilla, and beat until all the ingredients are thoroughly blended. Allow the mixture to thicken for a few minutes, then transfer it to a pastry bag *(technique, page 13)* made with a double thickness of parchment or wax paper.

Snip the pointed end off the pastry bag to make a ⅛-inch opening. Pipe a series of parallel lines, spaced ½ inch apart, within one of the marked circles; then pipe a second series of lines, at right angles to the first, to form a lattice pattern. Finally, pipe a scalloped edge around the outside of the circle to join up the ends of the piped lines. Pipe another three lattice rounds using the same technique.

Bake the lattice rounds until they are set and pale—about two minutes. Loosen them with a metal spatula and return them to the oven until they are pale gold around the edges—one to two minutes more.

Have ready a small, warm bowl for shaping the rounds into baskets. Lift the rounds, one at a time, and lightly press them into the bowl. If the rounds begin to set before they have been shaped, return them to the oven for a few seconds. Cool the baskets on a wire rack. Make another four baskets with the remaining mixture; use the same parchment paper, but place it on a second, cool, baking sheet.

To prepare the filling, cut three ½-inch-wide strips of zest from one of the limes and slice them into needle-thin shreds. Boil them in a little water until they are tender—about three minutes. Drain the shreds and set them aside.

Grate the remaining zest from the limes and squeeze the juice. Beat together the egg yolks and sugar until the mixture is thick, then stir in the lime juice and grated zest. Sprinkle the gelatin over 2 tablespoons of water in a small bowl, and let it soften for two minutes. Place the bowl over a saucepan of simmering water and stir until the gelatin has dissolved. Beat the gelatin solution into the lime and egg yolks, and let the mixture stand until it begins to set—about 15 minutes at room temperature.

Beat the egg whites until they are stiff but not dry. Whisk the yogurt into the partly set lime mixture; fold in the egg whites until the mixture is evenly blended. Set aside until it has just set—15 to 20 minutes.

Spoon the lime filling into the baskets. Decorate the filled baskets with strawberry slices and the reserved shreds of lime zest.

Oatmeal Blueberry Galettes

Makes 10 galettes
Working (and total) time: about 1 hour and 30 minutes

Per galette:
Calories **115**
Protein **3g.**
Cholesterol **10mg.**
Total fat **5g.**
Saturated fat **3g.**
Sodium **20mg.**

2 egg whites
7 tbsp. confectioners' sugar, sifted
¼ cup rolled oats
¼ cup unbleached all-purpose flour, sifted
2 tbsp. unsalted butter, melted and cooled
30 fresh blueberries, picked over and stemmed, to decorate
30 small petals cut from thin strips of orange zest to decorate
Creamy blueberry filling
⅔ cup plain low-fat yogurt
1 tbsp. confectioners' sugar, sifted
1 tsp. finely grated orange zest
10 oz. fresh blueberries, picked over and stemmed

Preheat the oven to 400° F. Line two baking sheets with parchment paper. Draw six 3-inch circles in pencil, spaced well apart, on each sheet of paper and invert them so that the marks face downward.

Beat the egg whites in a clean, grease-free bowl until they are white and frothy. Add 5 tablespoons of the confectioners' sugar and whip until it is dissolved, then beat in the rolled oats and flour. Finally, pour in the melted butter and beat the mixture thoroughly. Place a teaspoonful of the mixture in the middle of each circle on the parchment paper; using a small metal spatula, spread the mixture within the circles.

Bake the rounds until they are golden at the edges—three to four minutes. Let them rest on the parchment paper for 30 seconds, then lift them off with a metal spatula and cool them on a wire rack. Repeat the procedure, reusing the parchment paper for each batch, until the mixture is used up. There should be a total of 30 rounds.

To make the filling, mix together the yogurt, confectioners' sugar, and orange zest, then gently stir in the blueberries.

Assemble the galettes about 30 minutes before serving. Place one round on a work surface, spread it with a little filling, and cover with another round; spread this with more filling and top the assembly with a third round. Make up the rest of the rounds and filling into galettes in the same way. Sift the remaining 2 tablespoons of confectioners' sugar over the tops of the galettes, and decorate each one with 3 blueberries and 3 orange-zest petals.

EDITOR'S NOTE: *Any soft fruit in season, or a mixture of summer berries, can replace the blueberries.*

Preheat the oven to 375° F. Butter twelve 3-inch individual ring molds, dust them lightly with flour, and place them on a baking sheet.

Following the method on page 11, prepare a sponge-cake mixture using the ingredients listed below, left. Fill each ring mold almost to the top with the mixture, and bake the cakes until they are well risen, lightly browned, and springy to the touch—10 to 15 minutes. Carefully unmold the sponge cakes onto a wire rack to cool.

Put the 2 tablespoons of sugar and kirsch into a small, nonreactive saucepan with 2 tablespoons of cold water, and heat on low. When the sugar has dissolved, boil the syrup rapidly for one minute, then remove it from the heat.

Cut each ring cake in half horizontally, keeping matching pairs together, cut sides turned up. Brush each cut surface with a little of the kirsch syrup.

To make the filling, beat together the egg white, sugar, kirsch, and cream until the mixture will hold a peak. Spoon the filling into a pastry bag fitted with a ¼-inch star tip. Pipe the cream decoratively over the bottom half of each cake, and replace the tops. Sift the confectioners' sugar over the cakes, then pipe a whirl of cream into their centers. Decorate the cakes with the sugar-frosted rose and freesia petals.

Petal Ring Cakes

Makes 12 cakes
Working time: about 50 minutes
Total time: about 1 hour and 10 minutes

Per cake:
Calories **140**
Protein **2g.**
Cholesterol **60mg.**
Total fat **8g.**
Saturated fat **4g.**
Sodium **25mg.**

2 tbsp. sugar
2 tbsp. kirsch
1 tbsp. confectioners' sugar
12 sugar-frosted rose petals (box, right)
12 sugar-frosted freesia petals (box, right)
Sponge cake
2 eggs
1 egg white
¼ cup sugar
¾ cup unbleached all-purpose flour
1 tbsp. unsalted butter, melted and cooled
Kirsch cream filling
1 egg white
1 tsp. sugar
1 tsp. kirsch
⅔ cup whipping cream

Sugar-Frosted Petals

APPLYING A COATING. Beat an egg white until it lightens without foaming. Brush violet, primrose, freesia, or—as here—rose petals with the white, then dip them in superfine sugar. Transfer the petals to a plate and leave them in a warm place until they are dry and hard. In an airtight container, they will keep for weeks.

Harlequins

Makes 24 harlequins
Working time: about 1 hour and 10 minutes
Total time: about 2 hours (includes chilling)

Per harlequin:
Calories **60**
Protein **1g.**
Cholesterol **20mg.**
Total fat **2g.**
Saturated fat **1g.**
Sodium **10mg.**

3 peaches, halved and pitted
2½ cups fresh raspberries
2½ cups fresh black currants, ends removed, or blueberries
3 tbsp. sugar
2 tbsp. powdered gelatin
6 tbsp. plain low-fat yogurt
peach slices, raspberries, and black currants or blueberries to decorate
Sponge cake
2 eggs
1 egg white
⅓ cup sugar
¾ cup unbleached all-purpose flour
1 tbsp. unsalted butter, melted and cooled

Following the method on page 11, prepare a sponge cake with the ingredients listed above; bake the cake for 10 to 15 minutes only, then unmold and cool it.

Put the peaches, raspberries, and black currants or blueberries into three separate nonreactive saucepans, each with 2 tablespoons of water and 1 tablespoon of the sugar. Cook them over low heat, shaking the pans

occasionally, until the fruit is tender—three to four minutes. Purée each type of fruit separately in a food processor or a blender. Sieve each purée and keep them separate.

Sprinkle the gelatin over 6 tablespoons of water in a bowl and let it soften for two minutes. Place the bowl over a saucepan of simmering water and stir until the gelatin has completely dissolved. Stir one-third of the gelatin solution into each fruit purée, then beat 2 tablespoons of the yogurt into each. Chill the fruit mixtures in the refrigerator until they just begin to set—10 to 15 minutes.

Meanwhile, take the baking pan in which the cake was cooked, and line the bottom with a piece of foil long enough to stand 1½ inches above the rim of the pan on the two short sides; this will ease removal of the finished assembly later. Replace the cake.

Spread the black-currant or blueberry mixture evenly over the sponge cake, then chill it for five minutes to firm it up. Spread a peach layer over the black-currant or blueberry layer and chill again, then repeat with the raspberry mixture. Chill until the fruit layers have set firmly—at least 30 minutes.

Holding the aluminum-foil "handles," lift the sponge cake out of the pan. Carefully peel back the foil and trim the edges of the assembly, then cut the cake into diamonds, triangles, or squares, and arrange them on a serving plate. Decorate the top of each harlequin with pieces of fruit.

Red-Currant Charlottes

Makes 12 charlottes
Working time: about 1 hour
Total time: about 3 hours and 15 minutes

Per charlotte:
Calories **220**
Protein **5g.**
Cholesterol **60mg.**
Total fat **6g.**
Saturated fat **3g.**
Sodium **20mg.**

2 cups fresh red currants or raspberries, picked over, or frozen red currants or raspberries, thawed
4 tbsp. crème de cassis
¾ cup plain low-fat yogurt
2 tbsp. sugar
2½ tsp. powdered gelatin
1 sponge cake (recipe, page 11)
1 cup confectioners' sugar
red currants or raspberries for decoration

First, make the mousse for the filling. Purée the red currants or raspberries in a food processor or a blender; if you are using raspberries, press the purée through a sieve. Then add the crème de cassis, yogurt, and sugar, and process until the mixture is smooth—about 30 seconds. Sprinkle the gelatin over 2 tablespoons of water in a small bowl. Let it soften for two minutes, then place the bowl over a pan of simmering water and stir until the gelatin has completely dissolved. Add the gelatin solution to the fruit mixture and process for 20 seconds more. Set the mousse aside while you prepare the molds.

Line the bottoms of twelve ¼-cup soufflé molds with a circle of parchment paper. Oil the sides of the molds with a little safflower oil or other flavorless oil.

Trim off the outer crusts from the rectangle of sponge cake, and using a long, sharp knife, cut the cake in half horizontally. Using the top of a soufflé mold, stamp out 12 sponge circles from one of the sheets, then cut 12 smaller rounds that will fit in the bottom of the molds. Cut the remaining sponge cake into thin finger slices that are approximately 1 inch wide and long enough to line the soufflé molds from bottom to top.

Place the small sponge rounds in the bottoms of the molds. Using a rolling pin, flatten each sponge finger, then line the molds with the fingers, removing any surplus that overhangs the top. Do not worry if there are gaps in the lining of the molds—the mousse will fill these in and show through in stripes.

Fill each lined mold with mousse until it is level with the top. Lightly place a sponge-cake circle on top of each, then refrigerate the charlottes for at least one and a half hours.

Just before serving time, loosen the sides of each charlotte with a thin knife and turn them out onto a serving plate. Remove the circle of lining paper.

Prepare an icing by mixing the confectioners' sugar with 4 teaspoons of water until the mixture is smooth. Apply the icing with a small metal spatula and allow it to drip down the sides of the charlottes. Decorate the charlottes with the red currants or raspberries.

Pear and Fig Slices

Makes 16 slices
Working time: about 2 hours
Total time: about 6 hours (includes chilling)

Per slice:
Calories **150**
Protein **4g.**
Cholesterol **45mg.**
Total fat **3g.**
Saturated fat **1g.**
Sodium **50mg.**

1 tsp. fresh lemon juice
2 tbsp. vanilla sugar, or 2 tbsp. sugar mixed with ½ tsp. pure vanilla extract
1 lb. firm pears, peeled, cored, and sliced lengthwise into ½-inch slices
1 sponge cake (recipe, page 11), baked in a 15-by-10-inch pan for 20 to 25 minutes
5 fresh figs, peeled, sliced lengthwise into eighths
1 tbsp. confectioners' sugar, sifted
½ tsp. cocoa powder
Custard mousse
1¼ cups skim milk
½ vanilla bean, split
3 tbsp. cornstarch
2 egg whites
½ cup sugar
1 tbsp. lemon juice
2 tbsp. apple juice
1 tbsp. powdered gelatin
2 tsp. pure vanilla extract
2 tbsp. Marsala
¼ cup sour cream

Put the lemon juice and sugar into a pan with 1 cup of water, and bring to a boil. Lower the heat, add the pear slices, and poach them until they are soft and translucent—four to five minutes. Remove the pears from the liquid, let them cool to room temperature, then chill them in the refrigerator. Strain the poaching

syrup through a fine sieve, return it to the pan, and boil it until only 5 tablespoons remain. Set the syrup aside.

To make the custard mousse, heat the milk and the vanilla bean together over low heat. Blend the cornstarch with 2 tablespoons of the heated milk in a bowl. Scald the rest of the milk, then whisk it into the cornstarch. Return the mixture to the pan, bring it to a boil, beat it well, and simmer for five minutes more, stirring continuously. Remove the mixture from the heat. Strain it through a fine sieve, cover the surface closely with plastic wrap to prevent a skin from forming, and allow it to cool to room temperature.

Meanwhile, put the egg whites and sugar into a bowl set over a pan of simmering water; the bowl should not touch the water. Beat gently until the sugar has melted, then beat more vigorously until the mixture is thick and glossy and holds a trail across the surface. Remove the bowl from the saucepan, and beat the meringue until it cools to room temperature and is very stiff. Set the meringue aside.

Combine the lemon juice and apple juice in a small bowl, and sprinkle the gelatin on top. Allow the gelatin to soften for two minutes, then place the bowl over a saucepan of simmering water and stir until the gelatin has dissolved. Let it cool a little. Stir the vanilla extract and Marsala into the cooled milk mixture, then whisk in the dissolved gelatin. When the mixture is thick and creamy, blend the sour cream into it. Stir 1 tablespoon of meringue into the mixture until it is well blended, then gently fold in the rest of the meringue. Keep the custard mousse at room temperature while you prepare the mold.

Brush safflower oil, or another flavorless oil, over the bottom and sides of a 15-by-3-inch rectangular mold with removable sides. (If you do not have a mold with removable sides, you may use a 15-by-3-inch loaf pan lined with plastic wrap.) Line the bottom with a double thickness of parchment paper. Cut two strips from the sponge cake to fit exactly the dimensions of the prepared mold. Place one strip in the mold, press it down gently, and brush it with some of the reserved poaching syrup. Arrange the pear slices in a single layer on top of the sponge cake, and spread half the custard mousse on top. Chill for 20 minutes to let the custard set slightly. Arrange the sliced figs over the partly set custard, and spread the remaining custard mousse over the figs. Brush more poaching syrup over one side of the second sponge strip, and place it syrup side down on top of the custard. Cover the assembly with plastic wrap and press down lightly. Chill until the mousse has set—three to four hours.

Dust the surface of the sponge cake lightly with the confectioners' sugar. Cover each long edge with a 1-inch-wide strip of wax paper and sift the cocoa powder over the exposed center section. Slip a knife blade dipped in hot water around the edges of the assembly, then unmold it carefully. (If you are using a loaf pan lined with plastic, hold the edges of the wrap and carefully lift the cake from the pan.) Cut the cake into 16 slices and serve chilled.

Passionfruit Slices

Makes 16 slices
Working time: about 2 hours
Total time: about 6 hours (includes chilling)

Per slice:	
Calories **95**	1 egg
Protein **4g.**	2 tbsp. sugar
Cholesterol **45mg.**	¼ cup unbleached all-purpose flour
Total fat **1g.**	2 tbsp. apricot jam
Saturated fat **trace**	½ tbsp. brandy or unsweetened apple juice
Sodium **25mg.**	1½ tsp. powdered gelatin
	¾ cup clear unsweetened apple juice
	Passionfruit mousse
	2 eggs, separated
	½ cup plus 1 tbsp. sugar
	¼ cup unbleached all-purpose flour
	1½ tbsp. cornstarch
	1¼ cups skim milk
	1 tsp. pure vanilla extract
	10 passionfruit, halved
	1 tbsp. powdered gelatin
	1 tbsp. fresh lemon juice
	2 tbsp. unsweetened apple juice
	5 tbsp. sour cream

Preheat the oven to 350° F. Lightly butter a square cake pan that is 8 by 8 by 1½ inches, and line the bottom with parchment paper.

Make a sponge cake by beating together the egg and sugar in a bowl set over a saucepan of simmering water on very low heat. When the mixture is thick and foamy, remove the bowl from the saucepan, and continue beating until the mixture is cool and falls from the whisk in a thick, continuous ribbon. Sift the flour very lightly over the surface of the mixture, then fold it in gently using a large rubber spatula. Pour the batter into the prepared pan and spread it evenly. Bake the cake until it is springy to the touch and very slightly shrunk from the sides of the pan—8 to 10 minutes. Carefully turn the sponge cake out onto a wire rack and allow it to cool.

Next, make the passionfruit mousse. Beat the egg yolks with 2 tablespoons of the sugar until the mixture is thick, then fold in the flour and cornstarch. Scald the milk and vanilla extract together in a saucepan. Gradually whisk the scalded milk into the beaten egg yolks. Strain the mixture back into the saucepan and bring it to a boil, stirring constantly. Beat the custard well and simmer it for five minutes more, continuing to stir, then spoon it into a bowl and allow it to cool a little; cover the surface closely with plastic wrap to prevent a skin from forming.

Spoon the flesh and seeds of the passionfruit into a fine sieve, and press them with the back of a spoon to squeeze out all the juice. Reserve the juice and 1 teaspoon of the seeds; discard the rest.

Sprinkle the gelatin over the lemon juice and apple juice in a small bowl. Let the gelatin soften for two minutes, then set the bowl over a saucepan of simmering water and stir until the gelatin has completely dissolved. Warm the passionfruit juice in a saucepan, then stir in the gelatin solution. Cool the mixture to room temperature.

Meanwhile, put the egg whites and the remaining sugar into a bowl set over a pan of simmering water, taking care that the bowl does not touch the water. Beat gently until the sugar has melted, then beat more vigorously until the mixture is stiff and glossy. Remove the meringue from the heat.

Whisk the gelatin mixture into the custard, and when it is thick and creamy, stir in the sour cream. Stir 1 tablespoon of the meringue thoroughly into the custard, then gently fold in the rest. Keep the mousse at room temperature.

Line a 15-by-3-inch loaf pan with plastic wrap, allowing the wrap to extend 3 inches over the sides. Trim and cut the baked sponge cake to fit the bottom of the prepared pan, and press it firmly into position.

Heat the apricot jam until it is liquid, pass it through a sieve, then stir in the brandy or juice. Brush this mixture over the surface of the sponge cake. Pour the passionfruit mousse into the pan, and place it in the refrigerator until the mousse is fairly firm—approximately two hours.

Toward the end of the chilling time, make an apple-jelly glaze. Dissolve the gelatin in 2 tablespoons of the apple juice, as described above. Heat the remaining apple juice and stir in the dissolved gelatin. Let it cool, then chill until it has thickened slightly—10 to 15 minutes. Stir in the reserved teaspoon of passionfruit seeds. Carefully pour the apple jelly over the mousse.

(The seeds may be rearranged before the jelly sets.) Return the glazed mousse to the refrigerator to chill for an hour or two.

Lift the cake and plastic from the pan. Peel the plastic from the sides and then slide it out from under the cake. Cut the cake into 16 slices; serve chilled.

Espresso Cakes

Makes 8 cakes
Working (and total) time: about 25 minutes

Per cake:
Calories **225**
Protein **7g.**
Cholesterol **120mg.**
Total fat **8g.**
Saturated fat **4g.**
Sodium **55mg.**

1 sponge cake (recipe, page 11), 1 tsp. brandy added to uncooked batter
2 tbsp. brandy
4 tbsp. very strong black coffee (not instant coffee)
⅔ cup liqueur-flavored pastry cream (recipe, page 11), flavored with brandy
2 tbsp. cocoa powder
1 tbsp. coffee beans, finely ground
8 chocolate coffee beans

Trim off the four outer crusts from the edge of the cooked sponge cake. Using a long, sharp knife, cut the cake in half horizontally, making two large sheets. Combine the brandy and black coffee; using a pastry brush, lightly spread the mixture onto the cut surfaces of the sponge sheets. Cut each sheet crosswise through the center, making four rectangles in all.

Spread one-third of the brandy-flavored pastry cream over the cut surface of one of the rectangles, bringing it right up to the edges. Arrange a second sponge rectangle, cut side down, over the cream, followed by another third of the filling. Lay the third rectangle, cut side up, spread the last of the pastry cream over it, then set the final rectangle, cut side down, on top. Using a long, sharp knife, halve the assembly lengthwise, then cut each half crosswise into four equal pieces to give a total of eight cakes.

Place the espresso cakes in a straight line, and cover half of each one with a sheet of paper or thin cardboard. Sift the cocoa powder over the exposed half of each cake; the layer of cocoa powder should be fairly thick, or the liquid in the sponge cake will soak through and produce dark patches. Carefully move the paper or cardboard to cover the cocoa topping, and sift the finely ground coffee beans over the halves now exposed. Finally, decorate each espresso cake with a chocolate coffee bean.

Lime and Rum Sponge Cake

Makes 8 slices
Working time: about 25 minutes
Total time: about 55 minutes

Per slice:
Calories **215**
Protein **6g.**
Cholesterol **90mg.**
Total fat **7g.**
Saturated fat **3g.**
Sodium **50mg.**

1 sponge cake (recipe, page 11), finely grated zest of 2 limes added to uncooked batter
juice of 3 limes
3½ tbsp. white rum
⅔ cup plain low-fat yogurt
1¼ cups plus ½ tbsp. confectioners' sugar
lime slices to decorate
coconut shavings, briefly toasted under a hot broiler, to decorate

Trim the four outer crusts from the edges of the cake. Combine two-thirds of the lime juice with 3 table-spoons of the rum. Using a pastry brush, lightly spread the rum and lime mixture over the top of the cake.

Mix the yogurt with the remaining rum and the ½ tablespoon of sugar. Cut the cake crosswise into three equal rectangles. Layer the rectangles, one on top of another, with the flavored yogurt; the finished assembly will have three layers of cake and two of filling.

To make the icing, sift the 1¼ cups of confectioners' sugar into a bowl and stir in the remaining third of the lime juice, adding a little water, if necessary. Beat the icing until it is smooth and coats the back of a spoon. Carefully spread the icing over the top of the cake and allow it to almost set. Lightly score the top into eight equal portions. Decorate each one with halved slices of lime and with toasted coconut shavings. Allow the icing to set firmly before you slice the cake.

EDITOR'S NOTE: *Use a vegetable peeler to cut coconut shavings, slicing them from the outer surface of a peeled coconut.*

Chocolate-Mousse Layered Sponge Cake

Makes 20 slices
Working time: about 45 minutes
Total time: about 1 hour and 45 minutes

Per slice:
Calories **90**
Protein **3g.**
Cholesterol **35mg.**
Total fat **3g.**
Saturated fat **1g.**
Sodium **40mg.**

3 egg yolks
½ cup vanilla sugar, or ½ cup sugar mixed with ½ tsp. pure vanilla extract
4 egg whites
1 cup unbleached all-purpose flour
Chocolate-mousse filling
½ tsp. powdered gelatin
3½ oz. semisweet chocolate, chopped
⅓ cup low-fat ricotta cheese, sieved
2 egg whites

Preheat the oven to 350° F. Grease a 10-by-10-inch baking pan; line the bottom with parchment paper.

To make the sponge cake, put the egg yolks and 6 tablespoons of the sugar into a bowl. Place the bowl over a saucepan of hot but not boiling water set over low heat. Beat the eggs and sugar together with an electric hand-held mixer until the mixture is thick and very pale. Remove the bowl from the pan, and continue beating until the mixture is cool and falls from the beater in a ribbon. In a separate bowl, using a clean beater, beat the egg whites until they are stiff, sprinkle on the remaining sugar, and beat again until the mixture becomes glossy. Sift one-third of the flour over the egg-yolk mixture, add one-third of the egg whites, and gently but quickly fold them in using a rubber spatula. Add the remaining flour and egg whites in two more batches, using the same technique.

When all the ingredients are evenly combined, pour the batter into the prepared pan, and bake it until the cake is well risen, springy to the touch, and very slightly shrunk from the sides of the pan—25 to 30 minutes. Carefully unmold the cake onto a wire rack covered with wax paper. Allow it to cool for two or three minutes, then gently loosen the lining paper, but do not remove it. Place another wire rack over the bottom of the cake, and invert both racks together so that the sponge cake is right side up. Remove the top rack and let the cake cool while you prepare the filling.

Sprinkle the gelatin over 1½ tablespoons of water in a small bowl. Let it soften for two minutes, then place the bowl over a pan of simmering water and stir until the gelatin has completely dissolved. Melt the chocolate in a large flameproof bowl placed over a pan of hot but not boiling water. Remove the bowl from the heat, and while the chocolate is still warm, gradually beat in the ricotta, maintaining a smooth consistency. Gradually beat the gelatin solution into the chocolate mixture. Beat the egg whites until they are stiff, then lightly fold them into the mixture. Let the mousse set—about 30 minutes.

Using a long, sharp knife, trim the edges off the sponge cake and cut it in half lengthwise. Cut horizontally through each piece to make a total of four thin rectangles. Spread one-third of the chocolate filling over the cut surface of one sponge rectangle, and place another, cut side down, on top. Spread this with one-third of the filling, and cover it with another rectangle of cake, cut side up. Repeat with the remaining filling and final layer of sponge cake, placed cut side down. Press the layers lightly together.

To serve, cut the assembly widthwise into 10 thin fingers, then cut across these to make 20 slices.

Chocolate Mousse and Red-Currant Boxes

Makes 12 boxes
Working time: about 1 hour and 20 minutes
Total time: about 2 hours and 30 minutes
(includes chilling)

Per box:	
Calories **145**	*7 oz. semisweet chocolate*
Protein **3g.**	*½ tbsp. strong black coffee, cooled*
Cholesterol **40mg.**	*1 egg yolk*
Total fat **6g.**	*½ tbsp. brandy*
Saturated fat **3g.**	*2 egg whites*
Sodium **20mg.**	*2 cups red currants, ends removed*
	Fatless sponge cake
	1 egg
	1 egg white
	¼ cup sugar

½ cup unbleached all-purpose flour

First, make the chocolate mousse. Melt 2 ounces of the chocolate with the coffee in a large, flameproof bowl set over a pan of hot but not boiling water over low heat. Allow it to cool slightly, then stir in the egg yolk and the brandy. In a separate bowl, beat the egg whites until they are very stiff. Fold them into the chocolate mixture and allow the mousse to set in the refrigerator—about two hours—while you prepare the sponge and chocolate rectangles.

Preheat the oven to 350° F. Butter an 8-inch-square pan and line the bottom with parchment paper.

To make the sponge cake, put the egg, egg white, and sugar into a mixing bowl. Place the bowl over a saucepan of hot but not boiling water over low heat. Beat the eggs and sugar together by hand or with an electric hand-held mixer until the mixture is thick and very pale. Remove the bowl from the saucepan, and continue beating until the mixture is cool and falls from the whisk in a ribbon. Sift the flour very lightly over the surface of the beaten mixture, then fold it in gently using a large rubber spatula.

Pour the sponge mixture into the prepared pan and spread it evenly. Bake the cake until it is well risen, springy to the touch, and very slightly shrunk from the sides of the pan—20 to 25 minutes. Carefully turn the sponge cake out onto a wire rack. Loosen the baking paper, but do not remove it. Place another wire rack on top of the paper, then invert both racks together so that the cake is right side up on top of the paper. Remove the top rack and allow the cake to cool.

Grease a 13-by-9-inch square-cornered shallow baking pan and line the bottom with wax paper. Melt the remaining semisweet chocolate in a flameproof bowl set over a pan of hot water. Pour it into the prepared pan, spread it evenly with a metal spatula, and allow it to set in a cool place—approximately 30 minutes. Cut the chocolate *(technique, page 12)* into 36 rectangles, each measuring 3 by 1 inches. Cut 12 of the rectangles in half crosswise to make end pieces for the chocolate boxes.

Trim the crusts off the cake and slice it into twelve 3-by-¾-inch fingers. Using a metal spatula, spread a little of the mousse along the four sides of each sponge finger. Form little chocolate boxes by gently pressing the chocolate rectangles against the covered sides of the sponge fingers. Fill the boxes with the remaining mousse, and top them with a layer of red currants. Carefully transfer the boxes to serving plates.

EDITOR'S NOTE: *Strawberries or raspberries may be used instead of red currants.*

White-Chocolate Coffee Rolls

Makes 16 rolls
Working time: about 1 hour
Total time: about 2 hours (includes chilling)

Per roll:
Calories **215**
Protein **5g.**
Cholesterol **40mg.**
Total fat **10g.**
Saturated fat **6g.**
Sodium **40mg.**

1 tbsp. powdered gelatin
½ cup strong black coffee, cooled
1 tsp. coffee-flavored liqueur
¾ cup plain low-fat yogurt
1 sponge cake (recipe, page 11), 2 tsp. very strong black coffee added to the uncooked batter
10 oz. white chocolate
1 oz. semisweet chocolate

Sprinkle the gelatin over 2 tablespoons of the coffee in a small bowl, allow it to soften for two minutes, then set the bowl over a pan of simmering water and stir until the gelatin has completely dissolved. Blend the remaining coffee with the coffee-flavored liqueur and the yogurt in a food processor or a blender until the mixture is smooth. Add the gelatin solution and process for 20 seconds more. Refrigerate the filling until it has set—one to one and a half hours.

Using a long, sharp knife, cut through the sponge cake horizontally to make two thin sheets of cake. Trim off any dry crusts. Cut each sheet in half lengthwise, then cut each strip crosswise into four to make a total of sixteen 4-by-3-inch rectangles. Place each rectangle between two sheets of parchment paper, and roll it a little with a rolling pin; this will flatten the sponge cake and prevent it from cracking when it is rolled up with the filling.

Spread the cut side of each sponge rectangle with an even layer—about ¼ inch deep—of the coffee filling, keeping it away from the edges. Roll up each rectangle, starting from a short side, to make a tightly rolled cake.

To ice the rolls, melt the white chocolate in a flame-proof bowl set over a saucepan of simmering water. Place a roll on a narrow metal spatula, seam side down. Hold it over the bowl of white chocolate, and spoon the chocolate over the roll, covering it completely. Place the iced roll on a sheet of parchment paper. Repeat until all the rolls have been coated.

Melt the semisweet chocolate over hot water as described above, and spoon it into a wax-paper or parchment-paper pastry bag *(technique, page 13)*. Decorate the rolls with zigzags of fine chocolate piping. Allow the chocolate to set before you serve the coffee rolls.

Chocolate-Orange Roulades

Makes 16 roulades
Working time: about 1 hour
Total time: about 1 hour and 30 minutes

Per roulade:
Calories **195**
Protein **4g.**
Cholesterol **60mg.**
Total fat **8g.**
Saturated fat **5g.**
Sodium **25mg.**

10 oz. semisweet chocolate
1 egg yolk
1 tsp. orange-flavored liqueur
2 egg whites
1 sponge cake (recipe, page 11), substituting ¼ cup of cocoa powder for ¼ cup of flour
½ oz. hazelnuts, toasted and peeled (technique, page 29), chopped (about 2 tablespoons)

Melt 2 ounces of the chocolate in a flameproof bowl set over a saucepan of simmering water. Allow it to cool slightly, then stir in the egg yolk and liqueur. In a separate bowl, beat the egg whites until they are very stiff, then fold them into the chocolate. Refrigerate the mousse until it has set—about 30 minutes.

Using a long, serrated knife, cut through the sponge cake horizontally to make two thin sheets. Trim off any dry crusts. Cut each sheet in half lengthwise, then cut each strip crosswise into four to make a total of sixteen 4-by-3-inch rectangles. Place each rectangle between two sheets of parchment paper, and roll it a little with a rolling pin; this will flatten the sponge cake and prevent it from cracking when it is rolled up with the chocolate-orange mousse.

Spread the cut surface of each rectangle with an even layer of chocolate mousse about ¼ inch thick; do not spread the mousse right up to the edges of the cake. Working from a short edge, roll up each rectangle into a small, tight roll.

Melt the remaining chocolate in a bowl set over hot water. Place a roulade, seam side down, on a narrow metal spatula. Hold it over the bowl and spoon the melted chocolate over the roulade. Place the coated roll on a sheet of parchment paper and sprinkle it with chopped hazelnuts. Coat the remaining roulades in the same way and allow them to set before serving. The roulades will lift easily from the parchment paper when they are cool.

Gooseberry-Meringue Sandwich Slices

Makes 10 slices
Working time: about 1 hour
Total time: about 1 hour and 50 minutes

Per slice:
Calories **210**
Protein **3g.**
Cholesterol **60mg.**
Total fat **8g.**
Saturated fat **4g.**
Sodium **120mg.**

5 tbsp. unsalted butter
5 tbsp. sugar
2 egg yolks
1 tsp. pure vanilla extract
1 cup unbleached all-purpose flour
1 tsp. baking powder
½ cup skim milk
Meringue topping
2 egg whites
6 tbsp. sugar
Gooseberry filling
2½ cups green gooseberries or 2½ cups blueberries, ends removed
7 tbsp. sugar
½ tsp. ground cinnamon
1 tbsp. arrowroot

Preheat the oven to 350° F. Line the bottom of a 9-by-13-inch pan with a piece of parchment paper long enough to stand 1½ inches above the rim of the pan on the two short sides.

Cream the butter and sugar together in a mixing bowl until the mixture is pale and fluffy. Add the egg yolks and the vanilla extract, and gradually blend them into the butter and sugar mixture; add 1 tablespoon of the flour if the mixture begins to curdle. Sift the remaining flour with the baking powder and fold them into the creamed mixture alternately with the milk. Mix to create a smooth dropping consistency, and spread the mixture evenly over the bottom of the lined pan.

To make the meringue topping, beat the egg whites until they form peaks. Add the sugar a tablespoon at a time, beating constantly after each addition until the mixture is again stiff and glossy. Top the sponge mixture with the meringue and spread it almost to the edges of the pan. Bake the cake until the meringue is lightly browned and firm to the touch—about 35 minutes. Using the parchment "handles," ease the cake onto a wire rack and let it cool to room temperature.

Meanwhile, make the filling. Halve the gooseberries or blueberries, and put them into a nonreactive pan with 2 tablespoons of water. Stir in the sugar and cinnamon, and cook the berries over very low heat until they are tender but not mushy—10 to 15 minutes. Remove the berries with a slotted spoon and set them aside. Reserve 4 tablespoons of the juice in the pan and discard any excess. In a bowl, blend the arrowroot with 1 tablespoon of water and stir in the reserved juice. Return this mixture to the pan and cook over low heat until the juices begin to thicken. Add the berries; cook until the juice is clear and thick. Let the filling cool to room temperature—about 45 minutes.

Trim the edges of the cooled meringue cake and halve it lengthwise. Spread the berry filling evenly over the meringue topping of one half of the cake. Carefully place the other half—meringue side up—on top of the berries and press it down gently. Cut the cake into 10 slices and serve it as soon as possible.

EDITOR'S NOTE: *Frozen berries may be used instead of fresh. There is no need to thaw them first; simply increase their cooking time in the sugar syrup to 20 to 25 minutes.*

Coconut Meringue Fingers

Makes about 36 fingers
Working time: about 30 minutes
Total time: about 1 hour and 30 minutes

Per finger:
Calories **25**
Protein **trace**
Cholesterol **0mg.**
Total fat **1g.**
Saturated fat **trace**
Sodium **5mg.**

2 egg whites
½ cup vanilla sugar, or ½ cup sugar mixed with ½ tsp. pure vanilla extract
2 oz. finely shredded unsweetened coconut

Preheat the oven to 250° F. Line two baking sheets with parchment paper.

Put the egg whites and vanilla sugar into a large, flameproof bowl. Set the bowl over a pan of simmering water, taking care that the bottom of the bowl does not touch the water, and beat with an electric hand-held mixer until the egg whites form soft peaks—approximately five minutes. Remove the bowl from the heat, and continue beating the mixture at high speed until the meringue is stiff and glossy.

Using a rubber spatula, lightly fold in all but 2 tablespoons of the finely shredded coconut. Spoon the mixture into a pastry bag fitted with a ½-inch plain tip, and pipe out straight lines about 4 inches long on the prepared baking sheets. Sprinkle the remaining coconut over the tops of the fingers, then bake them until they are crisp, dry, and still white on the outside— about one hour. The meringue will still be slightly moist in the center. Carefully transfer the fingers to a wire rack to cool.

EDITOR'S NOTE: *These fingers may be stored in an airtight container for four to five days.*

Chocolate-Dipped Meringue Fingers

Makes 60 fingers
Working time: about 35 minutes
Total time: about 2 hours

Per finger:
Calories **35**
Protein **trace**
Cholesterol **0mg.**
Total fat **2g.**
Saturated fat **1g.**
Sodium **10mg.**

2 egg whites
½ cup sugar
1 tbsp. cocoa powder
½ tsp. grated orange zest, thoroughly dried on paper towels
5 oz. semisweet chocolate
5 oz. white chocolate

Preheat the oven to 250° F. Line two baking sheets with parchment paper.

Beat the egg whites until they form soft peaks. Add half the sugar, and continue beating until the mixture is stiff and glossy. Using a rubber spatula, gently fold in the remaining sugar. Divide the stiffly beaten egg whites into two equal parts. Flavor one half of the mixture with the cocoa powder and the other with the orange zest, folding the latter in very gently so as not to break the meringue.

Transfer one of the meringue mixtures to a pastry bag fitted with a ½-inch plain tip. Pipe 3-inch fingers, spaced at least 1 inch apart, onto one of the prepared baking sheets. Repeat the process with the second batch of meringue. Bake the fingers until they are completely dry—about one hour—then transfer them to wire racks to cool.

Melt the semisweet chocolate with 4 tablespoons of water in a flameproof bowl set over a pan of simmering water. Ice one side of the orange-flavored fingers by dipping them at an angle into the melted chocolate. Let them set on a sheet of parchment paper. Meanwhile, melt the white chocolate and coat the cocoa-flavored fingers in the same way.

EDITOR'S NOTE: *Meringue fingers may be stored in an airtight container in a cool, dry place for several days.*

A Trio of Meringues

Makes 24 meringues
Working time: about 1 hour
Total time: about 4 hours

Per plain meringue:
Calories **80**
Protein **2g.**
Cholesterol **0mg.**
Total fat **2g.**
Saturated fat **1g.**
Sodium **60mg.**

Per coconut meringue:
Calories **95**
Protein **2g.**
Cholesterol **0mg.**
Total fat **4g.**
Saturated fat **3g.**
Sodium **60mg.**

Per raspberry meringue:
Calories **80**
Protein **1g.**
Cholesterol **0mg.**
Total fat **2g.**
Saturated fat **1g.**
Sodium **60mg.**

4 egg whites
1 cup sugar
1½ oz. finely chopped unsweetened coconut, lightly toasted
¼ cup raspberries, puréed and sieved
1 oz. semisweet chocolate, finely grated
1 oz. walnuts, finely chopped (about ¼ cup)
Lemon-cheese filling
⅔ cup part-skim ricotta cheese
2 lemons, finely grated zest only
2 tbsp. sugar

Preheat the oven to 200° F. Line three baking sheets with parchment paper.

In a large bowl, beat the egg whites until they are stiff but not dry. Beat in the sugar, a little at a time, beating constantly between each addition until the meringue is very stiff and shiny.

Put one-third of the meringue into a pastry bag fitted with a 12-point ½-inch star tip. Put another third of the meringue into a small bowl and mix in two-thirds of the toasted coconut, then spoon the meringue into a pastry bag fitted with a ⅝-inch plain tip. Fold the raspberry purée into the remaining meringue, then spoon it into a pastry bag fitted with a 7-point ½-inch star tip.

Pipe the plain meringue in a continuous spiral pattern to form twelve 2½-inch lengths on one lined baking sheet; pipe the mixture in arcs that increase in size toward the center and decrease toward the end. Pipe the coconut meringue in 16 rounded mounds about 2 inches in diameter on the second baking sheet. Finally, pipe the raspberry-flavored meringue onto the third sheet to form 20 whirls that are about 2 inches in diameter. Bake the meringues until they are crisp and dry: The coconut ones need about two hours, the others from two and a half to three hours. If the meringues begin to brown before they are crisp, lower the oven temperature. Allow the meringues to cool on the baking sheets before you remove them from the paper.

To make the filling, beat the ricotta cheese in a bowl with the lemon zest and sugar until the mixture is smooth. Just before serving the meringues, sandwich them together in matching pairs with the lemon cheese. Sprinkle the plain meringues with the grated chocolate, the coconut meringues with the remaining ½ ounce of toasted coconut, and the raspberry meringues with the chopped walnuts.

EDITOR'S NOTE: *To toast coconut, heat it under the broiler for a minute or two, turning it frequently with a spoon until it turns golden brown.*

Chestnut Mocha Mountains

Makes 10 mountains
Working time: about 1 hour and 30 minutes
Total time: about 6 hours

Per mountain:
Calories **200**
Protein **3g.**
Cholesterol **0mg.**
Total fat **4g.**
Saturated fat **2g.**
Sodium **50mg.**

3 egg whites
¾ cup sugar
1 tbsp. cocoa powder
2 tsp. very finely ground coffee beans
15 oz. fresh chestnuts, peeled (technique, page 51)
½ vanilla bean, split
1¼ cups skim milk
7 tbsp. light brown sugar
2 to 3 tbsp. brandy or dark rum
½ tsp. finely grated orange zest
1½ oz. semisweet chocolate
2 oranges, segmented (technique, page 41) and coarsely chopped
5 tbsp. plain low-fat yogurt

Preheat the oven to 200° F. Line a baking sheet with parchment paper.

Put the egg whites and sugar into a large, flameproof bowl. Set the bowl over a pan of simmering water, taking care that the bottom of the bowl does not touch the water, and stir the mixture with a whisk until the sugar has dissolved and the mixture is hot—approximately five minutes. Remove the bowl from the heat and beat the mixture vigorously until peaks begin to form. Stir in the cocoa powder and the ground coffee beans, and beat again, briefly, until the meringue is stiff and glossy.

Transfer the meringue to a pastry bag fitted with a ½-inch plain tip, and pipe it in two stages, which will be easier than in one. Pipe 10 closed-up coils of meringue, each about 3 inches in diameter, onto the prepared baking sheet. These coils form the bases of the meringue cases. To make the walls that will enclose the filling, pipe two rings of meringue around the edge of each coil; alternatively, fit the pastry bag with a ½-inch star tip, and pipe small shell shapes, about ½ inch high, all the way around the edge of each base. Cook the meringue nests until they are firm to the touch and can be lifted easily from the paper—about four hours. Transfer them to a wire rack to cool.

Meanwhile, make the chestnut filling. Put the peeled chestnuts, vanilla bean, and milk into a heavy-bottomed saucepan. Bring to a boil, then lower the heat and simmer gently until the chestnuts are very soft—25 to 30 minutes. Remove the chestnuts with a slotted spoon. Remove and rinse the vanilla bean. Force the chestnuts through a sieve or reduce them to a coarse paste in a food processor.

Dissolve the light brown sugar in a saucepan with 5 tablespoons of water. Add the vanilla bean, and boil until the syrup is thick and lightly caramelized—about three minutes. Remove the vanilla bean and cool the syrup for a minute before beating it into the puréed chestnuts. Add the desired amount of brandy or rum,

but do not allow the chestnut purée to become too sticky—you should be able to rice or pipe it easily. Stir in the orange zest.

Melt the chocolate in a flameproof bowl set over a saucepan of simmering water. Brush a little of the melted chocolate over the base of each meringue case and let it harden. Mix the oranges and yogurt together, and spoon the mixture into the cases.

Make a mound of chestnut vermicelli on top of each meringue by pressing the purée through a potato ricer. Drop the strands of chestnut directly into the nests from the press, using a small knife to cut the strands when enough mixture has been pressed through. Alternatively, use a pastry bag with a small plain tip, piping the purée directly into each nest in a winding pattern until a mound is formed.

The nests will keep a few hours. If you are not serving them immediately, cover them lightly with plastic wrap to prevent the strands of chestnut from becoming too dry.

Chocolate Meringue Leaves

Makes 12 leaves
Working time: about 1 hour and 15 minutes
Total time: about 3 hours and 15 minutes

Per leaf:
Calories **100**
Protein **3g.**
Cholesterol **20mg.**
Total fat **4g.**
Saturated fat **2g.**
Sodium **15mg.**

2 egg whites
½ cup sugar
2½ oz. semisweet chocolate, 1 oz. grated
½ cup chocolate-flavored pastry cream (recipe, page 11)

Preheat the oven to 200° F. Cut a leaf-shaped template—about 3½ inches long and 3 inches wide—from a piece of cardboard. Cut sheets of parchment paper to fit two baking sheets. Draw six leaves on each sheet by tracing around the template with a pencil; leave at least 1 inch between leaves. Invert the papers and press them onto greased baking sheets.

Beat the egg whites until they form soft peaks. Continue beating and add the sugar, a little at a time; be sure the mixture is stiff and glossy after each addition of sugar before adding any more. Using a rubber spatula, lightly fold in the grated chocolate.

Transfer the egg-white mixture to a pastry bag fitted with a ¼-inch plain tip, and pipe out 12 leaf shapes onto the prepared baking sheets *(box, right)*. Bake the leaves until they are dry and can be lifted off the paper—two to three hours. They will still be a little soft in the center because the chocolate prevents them from hardening completely. Allow them to cool on the parchment paper.

Meanwhile, make the chocolate filigree leaves. On a piece of white cardboard, draw a leaf shape about 1 inch shorter and narrower than the meringue template, and cut three 18-by-6-inch rectangles of wax paper. Melt the remaining 1½ ounces of chocolate in a flameproof bowl set over a saucepan of simmering water. Fold a wax-paper or parchment-paper pastry bag, fill it with the melted chocolate, and snip off the tip of the bag *(technique, page 13)*. Using the cardboard as a tracing guide, pipe four chocolate filigree leaves onto each rectangle of paper as demonstrated below. Allow the chocolate leaves to set.

To serve, fill each meringue leaf with chocolate-flavored pastry cream. Carefully peel the backing paper away from the filigree leaves and gently lay one on top of each meringue.

Chocolate Filigree Leaves

FINE-PIPING THE LEAVES. Place a rectangle of wax paper or parchment paper over the tracing guide, and hold it firmly with one hand. Trace the outline of the leaf with a fine line of piped chocolate. Then, starting at the tip, fill in the center of the leaf by piping back and forth in a continuous pattern of squiggles. Reposition the tracing guide before piping the next leaf.

Making Meringue Leaves

1 PIPING THE OUTLINES. Twist the top of the pastry bag closed, and exerting a firm steady pressure, pipe out the meringue to form leaf outlines, following the penciled guidelines.

2 FILLING IN THE CENTERS. Starting at the pointed end of each leaf, move the pastry bag back and forth horizontally to fill in the outline with rows of evenly piped meringue. Pipe a short stem onto the bottom of each leaf.

3 COMPLETING THE LEAVES. Pipe a series of dots around the outside of each leaf to form a border. Pipe a second stem on top of the first.

Hazelnut Scallops with Chocolate Icing

Makes 20 scallops
Working time: about 1 hour
Total time: about 8 hours and 30 minutes

Per scallop:
Calories **90**
Protein **1g.**
Cholesterol **trace**
Total fat **3g.**
Saturated fat **1g.**
Sodium **10mg.**

3 egg whites
¾ cup sugar
3 oz. hazelnuts, toasted and peeled (technique, page 29), and ground (about ⅔ cup)
2 oz. semisweet chocolate
1½ tsp. strong black coffee, cooled
½ tbsp. unsalted butter
¼ cup confectioners' sugar
1 tbsp. hazelnut-flavored liqueur or amaretto

Preheat the oven to 200° F. Line a large baking sheet with parchment paper.

Beat the egg whites until they are very stiff. Add the sugar, a little at a time, beating well between each addition until the meringue is stiff and glossy. Fold in the hazelnuts with a rubber spatula.

Transfer the meringue to a pastry bag fitted with a ¾-inch star tip, and pipe 40 scallop shapes onto the lined baking sheet. Bake until the meringues feel firm to the touch and can be lifted off the paper easily—about two and a half hours. Turn off the oven and allow the meringues to rest inside until they are cold and completely dry—about four hours, or overnight.

Melt the chocolate with the coffee in a flameproof bowl set over a pan of simmering water. Stir in the butter. Sift in the confectioners' sugar and beat well. Remove from the heat, allow to cool briefly, then stir

in the liqueur. Set the icing aside for a few minutes more, until it has thickened slightly. Sandwich pairs of meringues together with the icing, and dip the ends in the icing. Place the scallops on a sheet of parchment paper until the icing has set—about one hour; arrange them carefully in a serving dish.

Walnut Meringues with Rose-Water Cream and Strawberries

Makes 10 meringues
Working time: about 30 minutes
Total time: about 7 hours

Per meringue:	3 egg whites
Calories **155**	¾ cup sugar
Protein **2g.**	1½ oz. walnuts, chopped and lightly toasted
Cholesterol **15mg.**	
Total fat **8g.**	¼ tsp. rose water
Saturated fat **3g.**	½ cup whipping cream
Sodium **20mg.**	12 oz. strawberries, hulled and thinly sliced

Preheat the oven to 200° F. Line a baking sheet with parchment paper.

Beat the egg whites until they form soft peaks. Add the sugar, a little at a time, beating constantly after each addition until the mixture is stiff and glossy. With a large rubber spatula, gently fold in the chopped walnuts together with ⅛ teaspoon of the rose water.

Transfer the mixture to a pastry bag fitted with a ¾-inch star tip, and pipe 20 small whirls, each about 2 inches in diameter, onto the prepared baking sheet. Bake the walnut meringues until they can be lifted easily off the paper—approximately two and a half hours. Then turn off the oven, but leave the meringues inside until they are cold and completely dry—four hours, or overnight.

Just before serving, whip the cream until it is stiff, add the remaining ⅛ teaspoon of rose water, and gently fold in the strawberry slices. Sandwich pairs of meringues together with this filling.

EDITOR'S NOTE: *To toast walnuts, put them under a hot broiler for about a minute, shaking them often. You may substitute ¼ teaspoon of pure vanilla extract for the rose water.*

Pistachio Meringues

Makes 12 meringues
Working time: about 30 minutes
Total time: about 7 hours

Per meringue:
Calories **135**
Protein **2g.**
Cholesterol **15mg.**
Total fat **7g.**
Saturated fat **3g.**
Sodium **20mg.**

3 egg whites
¾ cup sugar
6 tbsp. pistachio nuts, peeled, 1½ tbsp. chopped, remainder cut into slivers
½ cup whipping cream
1 kiwi fruit, peeled and sliced, slices quartered

Preheat the oven to 200° F. Line two baking sheets with parchment paper.

Beat the egg whites until they form soft peaks. Add the sugar, a little at a time, beating constantly after each addition until the mixture is stiff and glossy. With a large rubber spatula, gently fold in the slivered pistachio nuts. Transfer the mixture to a pastry bag fitted with a 1-inch plain tip, and pipe a total of 24 small meringues, each about 2 inches in diameter, onto the prepared baking sheets.

Bake the meringues until they can be lifted easily off the paper—about two and a half hours. Turn off the oven and allow the meringues to rest in the oven until they are cold and completely dry—about four hours.

Just before serving, whip the cream in a bowl and use it to sandwich the meringues together in pairs; for a decorative effect, pipe the cream through a star tip. Decorate the meringues with the chopped pistachio nuts and kiwi quarters. Serve immediately.

EDITOR'S NOTE: *To peel pistachio nuts, simmer them in boiling water for one minute, drain them, and rub them briskly in a towel until they have shed their skins.*

Cherry-Chocolate Meringue Nests

Makes 8 nests
Working time: about 45 minutes
Total time: about 7 hours

Per nest:
Calories **145**
Protein **2g.**
Cholesterol **0g.**
Total fat **3g.**
Saturated fat **2g.**
Sodium **15mg.**

2 egg whites
½ cup sugar
1 oz. semisweet chocolate
1 tbsp. kirsch
½ cup plain low-fat yogurt
5 oz. cherries, pitted and halved
3 tbsp. cherry or raspberry jam
1 tsp. arrowroot

Preheat the oven to 200° F. Line a baking sheet with parchment paper, and using an oval cutter as a guide, pencil eight 3-by-2-inch ovals onto the paper; leave at least 1 inch between ovals. Turn the paper over so that the marked side is underneath.

Put the egg whites and sugar into a large bowl set over a pan of simmering water, taking care that the bowl does not touch the water. Stir the mixture with a whisk until the sugar has dissolved and the egg whites are hot—about four minutes—then beat more vigorously until the meringue is stiff and glossy.

Spoon the meringue into a pastry bag fitted with a ½-inch star tip, and make bases for the nests by filling in the penciled ovals on the baking paper with piped coils of meringue. To make the sides of the nests, pipe two layers—one on top of the other—around the edge of each base. Bake the nests until they are crisp and dry but not brown—five to six hours. Carefully transfer them to a wire rack to cool.

Melt the chocolate in a flameproof bowl set over a pan of simmering water. Carefully brush the base inside each nest with a thin layer of melted chocolate. Let the chocolate set.

Beat the kirsch into the yogurt, and when the chocolate has set, spoon the yogurt into the nests. Top the flavored yogurt with the halved cherries.

In a small, nonreactive saucepan, heat the jam with 2 tablespoons of water until it is liquid. Sieve the melted jam to remove any solids, then stir in the arrowroot. Return the mixture to the pan and bring it to a boil, stirring constantly. Remove the pan from the heat and allow the glaze to thicken before brushing it carefully over the cherries.

Fruit-Filled Meringue Baskets

Makes 8 baskets
Working time: about 45 minutes
Total time: about 3 hours and 45 minutes

Per basket:
Calories **85**
Protein **1g.**
Cholesterol **0mg.**
Total fat **0g.**
Saturated fat **0g.**
Sodium **15mg.**

⅓ cup sugar
2 tbsp. light brown sugar
2 egg whites
Fruit filling
¾ cup fresh raspberries
1 kiwi fruit, peeled, halved lengthwise, and sliced
½ cup green seedless grapes, halved
1¼ cups fresh strawberries, hulled and sliced
2 tbsp. kirsch or dry white wine

Preheat the oven to 200° F. Line a large baking sheet with parchment paper, and pencil eight 2½-inch squares on the paper, spaced at least 1 inch apart. Turn the paper over so that the marked side is underneath.

Sift together both kinds of sugar. Beat the egg whites until they form soft peaks. Continue beating and gradually add the sugar mixture, a tablespoon at a time; the mixture should be stiff and glossy after each addition of sugar. Transfer the meringue to a pastry bag fitted with a ½-inch star tip. First, pipe around the edge of each outlined square on the baking paper, then pipe back and forth across the squares to make bases for the baskets. Make sides for the baskets by piping a border, two layers high, around the edge of each base. Complete the baskets with a meringue star at each corner.

Cook the meringues until they are completely dry and can be lifted easily off the paper—two and a half to three hours. Cool them on a wire rack.

Put the raspberries, kiwi slices, grape halves, and strawberry slices into a bowl, and stir in the kirsch or wine. Allow the fruit to stand for at least 30 minutes, stirring occasionally.

Just before serving time, arrange the fruit decoratively in the baskets.

Spicy Pear Roulade

Serves 18
Working time: about 1 hour
Total time: about 8 hours (includes soaking and rising)

Calories **110**
Protein **2g.**
Cholesterol **15mg.**
Total fat **3g.**
Saturated fat **trace**
Sodium **60mg.**

1½ cups unbleached all-purpose flour

½ tsp. salt

½ tsp. ground cardamom

½ tsp. active dry yeast

2 tbsp. light brown sugar

6 tbsp. tepid skim milk

1 egg, lightly beaten

1 tbsp. walnut or safflower oil

1 tsp. sugar

Spicy pear filling

7 tbsp. fresh crumbs from dark pumpernickel
bread or gingerbread

2 tbsp. Calvados or dark rum

2 tbsp. dark brown sugar

1 tbsp. honey

1 tbsp. cocoa powder

1 tbsp. pumpkin pie spice

⅓ cup pecans, coarsely chopped

1 cup dried pears, soaked in water for at least 4 hours,
drained, and coarsely chopped

Sift the flour, salt, and cardamom together into a warm mixing bowl. Mix the yeast with 1 teaspoon of the light brown sugar and 5 tablespoons of the milk. Add ½ cup of the flour mixture to the yeast, and stir with a fork to form a soft paste. Set this mixture aside in a warm place to rise for about 30 minutes.

Form a well in the remaining flour mixture, and add the risen yeast, egg, oil, and remaining light brown sugar. Using a wooden spoon, blend the liquid ingredients well, then gradually draw in the flour. When the dough becomes too stiff to mix easily with the spoon, use your hands. Turn out the dough onto a floured surface, and knead until it is smooth, elastic, and not too sticky—about 10 minutes. Transfer the dough to a lightly oiled bowl and cover it with a piece of plastic wrap, then put the bowl in a warm place until the dough has doubled in volume—approximately one and a half hours.

Punch down the risen dough, turn it out onto a floured surface, and knead it for two to three minutes. Sprinkle more flour onto the work surface and the dough, then roll out the dough to form a rectangle about 15 by 12 inches.

To make the filling, moisten the crumbs with the Calvados or rum, and stir in the dark brown sugar. Spread the crumbs over the rectangle of dough, extending right to the edge on three sides but leaving a margin of 1 inch free of filling along one long edge. Drizzle the honey over the crumbs, sift on the cocoa and pumpkin pie spice, and sprinkle on the pecans. Arrange the pears in three rows parallel to the filling-free edge, stopping the rows 1 inch from the edge of the crumbs. Roll up the dough, starting with the long side that has been coated to the edge. Seal the ends by pressing them together. Place the roll, seam side underneath, on a lightly buttered baking sheet, tucking down the sealed ends.

Preheat the oven to 350° F., allowing the roulade to rise a little, loosely covered with plastic wrap, while the oven is warming. Just before you bake the roulade, dissolve the sugar in the remaining tablespoon of milk and brush this over the dough as a glaze. Bake the roulade until it is golden brown and sounds slightly hollow when tapped—35 to 45 minutes. Cool it on a wire rack; to make a soft crust, wrap the roulade in a dishtowel while it is still warm. Slice the roulade just before you serve it.

SUGGESTED ACCOMPANIMENT: *sour cream or yogurt.*

Brioche Peaches

Makes 10 peaches
Working time: about 1 hour and 30 minutes
Total time: about 7 hours and 45 minutes
(includes rising and cooling)

Per peach:
Calories **225**
Protein **5g.**
Cholesterol **65mg.**
Total fat **8g.**
Saturated fat **4g.**
Sodium **40mg.**

½ tsp. active dry yeast
3 tbsp. tepid skim milk
2¼ cups unbleached all-purpose flour
1 tbsp. sugar
⅛ tsp. salt
2 eggs, beaten
6 tbsp. unsalted butter, softened
sugar to decorate
angelica, cut into 20 small leaves, or 20 small fresh mint leaves

Almond cream filling

½ tsp. pure almond extract
1 egg white
3 tbsp. sugar
5 tbsp. sour cream

Apricot-raspberry glaze

2 tbsp. sugar
2 tbsp. white rum
2 tbsp. apricot jam
1 tbsp. raspberry jam

To make the brioche dough, dissolve the yeast in the tepid milk. Sift the flour, sugar, and salt into a mixing bowl, and make a well in the center. Pour the yeast liquid into the flour and add the eggs. Beat the ingredients together with a wooden spoon to form a soft dough. Transfer the dough to a lightly floured surface, and knead it by lifting it and slapping it down on the work surface until it becomes firm and elastic—10 to 15 minutes. Work the butter, a little at a time, into the dough. Place the dough in a clean bowl. Cover the bowl with plastic wrap, then refrigerate the dough for five hours to allow it to rise very slowly.

Lightly butter two large baking sheets. Turn out the risen dough onto a floured surface and punch it down to its original size. Knead lightly until the dough is smooth—two to three minutes. Shape the dough into a long sausage and cut it into 20 equal-size pieces. Shape each piece into a neat round and place the rounds on the buttered baking sheets, spaced well apart. Flatten each round slightly, then cover the baking sheets with plastic wrap. Leave them in a warm place until the rounds have doubled in size—about 30 minutes. Meanwhile, preheat the oven to 425° F.

Remove the plastic wrap and bake the brioches until they are well risen, golden brown, and sound hollow when tapped on the bottom—about 15 minutes. Transfer the brioches to wire racks to cool.

Meanwhile, make the almond cream filling. Put the almond extract, egg white, and sugar into a small bowl, and place the bowl over a saucepan of gently simmering water—the bottom of the bowl must not touch the water. Beat the egg white and sugar until the mixture is very thick and glossy. Remove the bowl from the heat and continue to beat the mixture until it is cool. Very gradually beat the sour cream into the meringue. Refrigerate until needed.

Using a small knife, cut out a small cone shape from the bottom of each brioche to make a hollow. Fill the hollows with almond cream, and sandwich pairs of brioches together to form peaches. Place the peaches on wire racks.

To make the glaze, put the sugar into a small saucepan with 4 tablespoons of cold water. Heat on low, stirring until every crystal of sugar is dissolved. Bring to a boil and cook for 30 seconds, then remove the pan from the heat and stir in the rum. Brush the hot syrup over the peaches. Heat the apricot and raspberry jams, in separate saucepans, until boiling, then sieve them to remove any solids. Brush the apricot jam over the peaches to coat them completely, then ''blush'' each one with a pastry brush dipped in the raspberry jam.

Sift a little sugar over the peaches, and decorate each one with 2 angelica leaves or 2 mint leaves. Place the brioches in paper cups for serving.

½ cup semolina flour, preferably coarsely ground	
5 tbsp. unsalted butter, melted	
2 tbsp. candied lemon peel, finely chopped (optional)	
1 tbsp. poppy seeds	
24 pecan halves	
Lemon-vodka syrup	
⅔ cup honey	
4 tbsp. fresh lemon juice	
4 tbsp. vodka	

Stir the yeast into the milk, add 1 tablespoon of the brown sugar, and stir well. Set the yeast solution aside until its surface becomes frothy—about 10 minutes. Stir in ½ cup of the all-purpose flour, and then leave the mixture in a warm place until it has doubled in volume—approximately 30 minutes.

In a small bowl, beat the egg yolks with the remaining sugar, the vanilla, and the lemon zest. Dissolve the saffron in the vodka and add it to the egg mixture. In a separate bowl, beat the egg whites with the salt until they are frothy and form soft peaks.

Sift the remaining all-purpose flour and the semolina into a warm mixing bowl. Pour in the yeast starter and the egg-yolk mixture, then beat the mixture with a wooden spoon until it forms a stiff mass. Beat in two-thirds of the egg whites, then fold in the remaining whites. Let the dough rest for 10 minutes, then knead it in the bowl for 10 minutes. Grease the surface of the dough lightly with a little of the melted butter, cover it with plastic wrap, and set it aside in a warm place. When the dough has doubled in volume—about 30 minutes—beat in the rest of the cooled melted butter, together with the candied lemon peel, if you are using it, and the poppy seeds. Knead the dough for a few minutes more.

Lightly butter and flour twenty-four ⅓-cup baba molds. Using a teaspoon, drop the dough into the baba molds, filling them no more than one-third full. Set the molds aside in a warm place until the dough has more than doubled in volume—30 to 45 minutes. Meanwhile, preheat the oven to 375° F.

Bake the babas until a skewer plunged to the bottom of the mold comes out clean—10 to 12 minutes. Unmold the babas immediately and cool them briefly on a wire rack.

To make the syrup, heat the honey and lemon juice in a nonreactive saucepan. When the mixture is hot, remove it from the heat and stir in the vodka. Trim the rounded wider ends of the babas so they will sit flat on a plate. Pierce the babas in two or three places with a skewer, then pour a little of the hot syrup over each one. Serve the babas warm or cold, with half a pecan on top to decorate.

EDITOR'S NOTE: *For variety, the babas can be decorated with a little sifted confectioners' sugar and served with yogurt.*

Poppy-Seed Babas

Makes 24 babas
Working time: about 1 hour and 15 minutes
Total time: about 3 hours (includes rising)

Per baba:	
Calories **145**	1 tsp. active dry yeast
Protein **3g.**	¾ cup tepid skim milk
Cholesterol **25mg.**	5 tbsp. light brown sugar
Total fat **5g.**	2½ cups unbleached all-purpose flour
Saturated fat **2g.**	2 eggs, separated
Sodium **95mg.**	1 tsp. pure vanilla extract
	½ lemon, grated zest only
	⅛ tsp. powdered saffron
	1 tbsp. vodka
	¼ tsp. salt

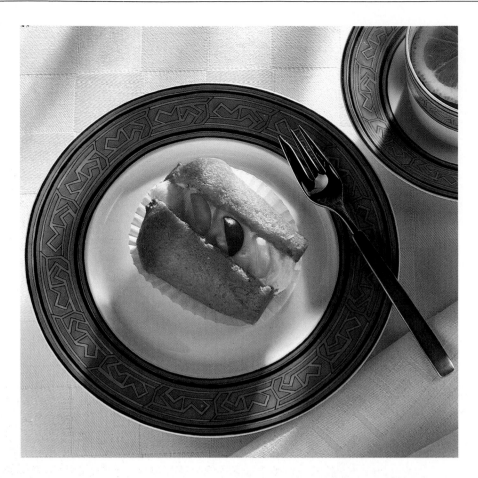

Lime and Ginger Babas

Makes 10 babas
Working time: about 1 hour and 30 minutes
Total time: about 3 hours and 30 minutes (includes rising)

Per baba:
Calories **220**
Protein **8g.**
Cholesterol **60mg.**
Total fat **7g.**
Saturated fat **4g.**
Sodium **110mg.**

½ tsp. active dry yeast
½ cup tepid skim milk
1½ tbsp. light brown sugar
2 cups unbleached all-purpose flour
½ tsp. salt
2 eggs, beaten
4 tbsp. unsalted butter, softened
Lime and ginger syrup
2 tbsp. light brown sugar
1½ tbsp. fresh lime juice
4 tbsp. syrup from preserved stem ginger
1½ tbsp. brandy
Ricotta and grape filling
¾ cup part-skim ricotta cheese
2 tbsp. honey
2 tsp. brandy
1 tsp. fresh lime juice
½ tsp. grated lime zest
1 tsp. pure vanilla extract
2 pieces preserved stem ginger (about 1 inch each), finely chopped
15 red or green grapes, or a mixture of both, halved and seeded

Stir the yeast into the milk, add 1 teaspoon of the sugar, and mix well. Set the yeast solution aside until the surface becomes frothy—10 to 15 minutes.

Sift the flour and salt into a warmed mixing bowl, and form a well in the center. Pour the yeast mixture and the eggs into the well, and mix with a wooden spoon, gradually drawing in the flour. When all the ingredients are combined, steady the bowl with one hand, and knead the dough with the other by lifting it and slapping it back into the bowl for 7 to 10 minutes. (The mixture will be too slack for conventional kneading.) Spread the softened butter over the surface of the dough, then cover the bowl and set it aside in a warm place until the dough has tripled in volume—about one hour.

Punch down the risen dough and sprinkle on the remaining sugar. Use your hand to mix in the butter and sugar, then knead the dough again, as described above, for two minutes. Lightly butter and flour ten ½-cup individual baba molds, and fill them halfway with the dough. Set them aside until the dough has risen to the tops of the molds—about 30 minutes. Meanwhile, preheat the oven to 375° F.

Bake the risen babas until they are brown and crisp on top and a skewer inserted into the center comes out clean—about 15 minutes. Turn them out immediately, crisp side down, onto a wire rack.

To make the syrup, put the sugar into a small, nonreactive saucepan with 2 tablespoons of water and boil for two minutes. Add the lime juice and ginger syrup, and return to a boil. Remove the pan from the heat and stir in the brandy. While the babas are still warm, pour the syrup into a shallow baking pan, large enough to contain all the babas in one layer. Add the babas, turning them quickly until all the syrup is absorbed.

To make the filling, beat the ricotta in a bowl until it is smooth. Stir in the honey, brandy, lime juice and zest, and vanilla, then fold in the chopped preserved ginger. With a sharp serrated knife, slice the babas in half lengthwise. Sandwich the halves back together with the filling, and place them in foil or paper cups. Arrange the grape halves on top of the ricotta and chill the babas slightly before serving them.

Apple Streusel Tart

Serves 24
Working time: about 1 hour
Total time: about 3 hours (includes rising)

Calories **100**
Protein **2g.**
Cholesterol **15mg.**
Total fat **2g.**
Saturated fat **1g.**
Sodium **40mg.**

⅓ tsp. active dry yeast
½ cup tepid skim milk
3 tbsp. light brown sugar
3 tbsp. unsalted butter, melted
1 egg, beaten
2 cups unbleached all-purpose flour
½ tsp. salt
4 cardamom pods, husks removed and seeds ground
4 medium tart apples
2 tbsp. apricot jam

Streusel

½ cup unbleached all-purpose flour
1 tsp. ground cinnamon
2 tbsp. light brown sugar
2 tbsp. unsalted butter, softened

Mix together the yeast, 3 tablespoons of the skim milk, and 1 teaspoon of the brown sugar. Leave the mixture in a warm place until its surface becomes frothy—10 to 15 minutes. Meanwhile, dissolve the rest of the sugar in the remaining milk, then stir in the butter and the beaten egg.

Sift the flour, salt, and ground cardamom into a large warmed mixing bowl. Form a well in the center of the dry ingredients, and pour in the yeast and the milk and egg mixture. Using a wooden spoon, blend the liquids together and gradually draw in flour until all the ingredients are well combined. Continue to beat with the wooden spoon until the dough is smooth and slightly elastic—two to three minutes—it will remain sticky. Cover the dough with plastic wrap and leave it in a warm place to rise until it has almost tripled in volume—about one hour.

Meanwhile, make the streusel. Combine the flour, cinnamon, sugar, and butter in a mixing bowl, and blend them together with your fingers until they form coarse crumbs. Set the mixture aside. Preheat the oven to 350° F. and lightly butter a baking sheet.

Turn out the risen dough onto a floured board and knead it until it is smooth—two to three minutes. Flatten the dough a little, dredge more flour over it, and roll it out to form a 12-by-8-inch rectangle. Transfer the dough to the prepared baking sheet.

Core, halve, and peel the apples, and cut them into thin slices. Arrange the slices in three parallel rows on top of the dough. Sprinkle the streusel around the edges and into the gaps between the rows. Bake the tart until the streusel is golden and the apples are soft—40 to 50 minutes.

While the tart is still warm, prepare a glaze. Mix the apricot jam with 2 tablespoons of water and bring it to a boil. Brush the apples with the glaze. Let the tart cool before you serve it.

Danish Pastries

Makes 26 pastries
Working time: about 1 hour and 10 minutes
Total time: about 3 hours and 15 minutes
(includes chilling and rising)

Per pastry:
Calories **75**
Protein **1g.**
Cholesterol **10mg.**
Total fat **4g.**
Saturated fat **2g.**
Sodium **20mg.**

¼ tsp. active dry yeast
2 cups unbleached all-purpose flour
¼ tsp. salt
1 tsp. sugar
8 tbsp. unsalted butter, chilled
1 egg white
2 tbsp. apricot jam
Fruit fillings
2 fresh figs, peeled and chopped, or 2 dried figs, chopped
4 apricots, peeled, halved, and pitted
2 nectarines or peaches, peeled, pitted, and sliced

Stir the yeast into ⅓ cup of warm water until it is dissolved. Sift the flour, salt, and sugar into a bowl. Cut 2 tablespoons of the butter into small pieces and add it to the bowl; chill the remaining butter until it is needed. With the fingertips, rub the butter into the flour until the mixture resembles fine breadcrumbs. Add the yeast and egg white to the flour mixture, and stir with a wooden spoon to make a soft dough. On a lightly floured surface, knead the dough until it is smooth, elastic, and no longer sticky—about 10 minutes. Place the dough in a plastic bag and refrigerate it for 30 minutes.

Roll out the dough to an oblong about 20 by 8 inches. Put the remaining butter between two sheets of wax paper, and roll into a thin oblong about 12 by 6 inches. Place the butter on the dough, covering about two-thirds of its length. Fold the unbuttered third over half of the buttered dough; fold over the remaining buttered section. With a rolling pin or your hands, press down well to seal the edges.

Give the dough a quarter turn. Roll out the dough lightly, continuing to roll until it is an oblong about 20 by 8 inches. Fold the dough into thirds again, cover it with plastic wrap, and refrigerate it for 20 minutes. Unwrap the dough, place it on a work surface with one of the short sides toward you, and roll it into an oblong about 20 by 8 inches. Fold the dough into thirds again, cover it with plastic wrap, and refrigerate it for 20 minutes. Repeat the turning, rolling, folding, and refrigerating twice more.

Roll out the dough to an oblong about 18 by 12 inches. Cut the dough crosswise into three different-size oblongs—12 by 4 inches, 12 by 6 inches, and 12 by 8 inches.

Spread the fresh or dried chopped figs over the smallest rectangle, roll it up into a firm roll, then slice into six spirals *(right, top)*. Place the spirals on a large baking sheet and cover them with a damp cloth or plastic wrap. Cut the 12-by-6-inch sheet of dough into eight 3-inch squares. Place an apricot half in the center of each square, make diagonal cuts from the corners to the edge of the apricot half, and fold alternate points into the center to form a windmill *(right, center)*. Place the pastries on the baking sheet and cover. Cut the remaining dough into six 4-inch squares, then cut each square in half diagonally to form a total of 12 triangles. Place 2 nectarine or peach slices on the longest edge of each triangle, roll up neatly, and turn the ends in to make a crescent shape *(right, bottom)*. Place the crescents on the baking sheet with the other pastries and cover.

Set the pastries aside until doubled in size—40 to 50 minutes. Preheat the oven to 450° F.

Bake the Danish pastries until they are golden brown and well risen—10 to 15 minutes. In the meantime, heat the apricot jam in a small, nonreactive saucepan until it is liquid, then pass it through a fine sieve. Transfer the pastries to a wire rack set over a tray; brush them with the warm glaze and let them cool for 15 to 20 minutes.

Making Spirals

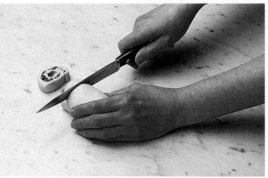

1 *ROLLING UP THE DOUGH AND FILLING. Starting from one of the short ends, roll up the dough and fig filling as you would a jelly roll. Keep the roll tight as you work, and ensure that the ends of the roll remain aligned.*

2 *SLICING THE ROLL. Place the roll seam side down on a work surface. With a sharp knife, cut the roll into six equal slices.*

Shaping Windmills

1 *CUTTING DIAGONAL LINES. Place an apricot half in the center of a 3-inch square of dough. With a sharp knife, cut a diagonal line from each corner to the edge of the apricot, so that you have four triangles joined in the middle.*

2 *FOLDING IN POINTS. Working in one direction, fold alternate points into the center, over the apricot. Press the final tip down firmly on top of the others to make a secure join.*

Forming Crescents

1 *ENCLOSING THE FRUIT. Place 2 nectarine or peach slices, one slightly overlapping another, along the longest side of a triangle of dough. Holding fruit and dough together, roll the base of the triangle toward the apex.*

2 *CURVING AROUND THE CRESCENT. Place the roll seam side down on the work surface. Gently shape both ends around to form a crescent.*

Raspberry Savarins

Makes 10 savarins
Working time: about 30 minutes
Total time: about 2 hours (includes rising)

Per savarin:
Calories **160**
Protein **3g.**
Cholesterol **40mg.**
Total fat **6g.**
Saturated fat **3g.**
Sodium **50mg.**

¼ tsp. active dry yeast
1¼ cups unbleached all-purpose flour
¼ cup plus 1 tbsp. sugar
¼ tsp. salt
1 egg
1 egg white
4 tbsp. unsalted butter, softened
1 vanilla bean, or ¼ tsp. pure vanilla extract
4 tbsp. eau de vie de framboise or kirsch
1½ cups fresh raspberries

Stir the yeast into 2 tablespoons of warm water and set the mixture aside until the yeast has dissolved—approximately five minutes.

Sift the all-purpose flour into a mixing bowl, blend in 1 tablespoon of the sugar and the salt, then make a well in the center. Lightly beat the egg and egg white together, and pour them into the well with the yeast solution. Using a wooden spoon, beat the ingredients until they have formed a smooth, slightly elastic dough—four to five minutes.

Cover the bowl with plastic wrap and put it in a warm place until the dough has risen to twice its original volume—about 30 minutes. Place the dough on a work surface and gradually work in the butter with your hands. Knead the dough until it is smooth—two to three minutes.

Preheat the oven to 400° F. Brush the insides of ten 3-inch ring molds with melted butter. Divide the dough among them and leave them in a warm place until the dough has risen to the top of the molds—20 to 30 minutes. Place the savarins on a baking sheet, and bake them until they are puffy and golden brown—about 15 minutes. Unmold them onto a wire rack set over a tray.

In a small, nonreactive saucepan, dissolve the remaining ¼ cup of sugar in ½ cup of water and bring it to a boil. Lower the heat, then add the vanilla and simmer for five minutes. Allow to cool. Stir in the *eau de vie* or kirsch.

Spoon the syrup over the savarins, respooning any that drips onto the tray below. Fill the centers with the fresh raspberries and serve.

Miniature Kugelhopfs

A TRADITIONAL KUGELHOPF IS BAKED IN A FANCY FLUTED MOLD THAT HAS A CENTRAL FUNNEL TO ENSURE THAT THE MIXTURE COOKS THROUGH EVENLY. FOR THESE SMALLER VERSIONS, THE FUNNEL IS UNNECESSARY.

Makes 12 kugelhopfs
Working time: about 1 hour
Total time: about 4 hours (includes rising)

Per kugelhopf:
Calories **165**
Protein **4g.**
Cholesterol **50mg.**
Total fat **5g.**
Saturated fat **3g.**
Sodium **20mg.**

⅓ cup raisins
½ tsp. active dry yeast
⅓ cup tepid skim milk
2¼ cups unbleached all-purpose flour
⅛ tsp. salt
2 tbsp. vanilla sugar, or 2 tbsp. sugar mixed with ¼ tsp. pure vanilla extract
2 eggs, beaten
2 tbsp. dark rum (optional)
4 tbsp. unsalted butter, diced and softened
3 tbsp. mixed candied peel, chopped
2 tsp. finely grated orange zest
2 tsp. finely grated lemon zest
confectioners' sugar to decorate

Put the raisins into a small bowl, pour boiling water over them, and let them soak for at least 30 minutes. Stir the yeast into the milk and leave it in a warm place until it is frothy—15 to 20 minutes.

Sift the flour and salt into a mixing bowl, stir in the vanilla sugar, and form a well in the center. Pour the eggs, rum, if you are using it, and yeast mixture into the well, then use a large wooden spoon or your hand to draw the ingredients together and form a smooth dough. Turn out the dough onto a lightly floured surface, and knead it well until it is firm and elastic— about 15 minutes. Gradually work the butter into the dough by first squeezing small pieces of butter between your fingers, then squeezing them into the dough. Continue until all the butter has been incorporated, then knead the dough until it is smooth—two to three minutes. Transfer it to a very lightly oiled bowl, cover the bowl with plastic wrap, and leave it in a warm place until the dough has doubled in volume—one and a half to two hours.

Drain the raisins well, then mix them with the candied peel and orange and lemon zest. Lightly butter twelve ¼-cup deep fluted molds. Turn the dough out onto a lightly floured surface and work in the fruit mixture with your hands, spreading it evenly throughout the dough. Divide the dough into 12 equal portions and place one in each mold, pressing the dough down. Cover the molds with plastic wrap and set them aside until the dough is well risen—about 30 minutes. Meanwhile, preheat the oven to 400° F.

Lower the oven temperature to 375° F. Bake the kugelhopfs until the tops are browned and the sides have shrunk slightly from the molds—about 20 minutes. Remove the kugelhopfs from the oven and unmold them onto a wire rack to cool. Sift a little confectioners' sugar over the surface of the kugelhopfs just before serving.

3 *Freshly baked ginger snaps, molded while they are hot and pliable, harden into delicate horns as they cool (recipe, page 116).*

Delicate Confections

An exquisite selection of petits fours presented with after-dinner coffee can tempt even the most diet-conscious guest into indiscretion—so if they are to be served as part of a meal, it is best to substitute them for an ordinary dessert. Alternatively, they make the perfect accompaniment to morning coffee or after-noon tea. Petits fours are an ideal standby for unex-pected visitors, since many can be stored for up to seven days, and most of them will keep for at least two or three days in an airtight container or in the refrig-erator. Prettily boxed, they make an ideal gift.

Petits fours, literally, means "little ovens"—that is, little baked goods. In classic French patisserie, these bite-size sweetmeats are divided into two main cate-gories—*riches* and *secs.* As their name implies, tradi-tional petits fours riches are sumptuous morsels, in-cluding such delights as tiny sponge shapes enrobed with fondant icing and decorated with sugar flowers and chocolate tracery. The iced sponge cakes on page 104 call for beaten fatless sponge cake and a thin layer of icing, but they lack nothing in visual appeal and richness of taste.

Petits fours secs are more cookielike in appearance and texture; on the following pages, you will find miniature versions of macaroons, florentines, snaps, and shortbread. Intermediate between these two cat-egories are cakes such as the pistachio and almond petits fours on page 115, which contain relatively little sugar and will appeal to those who do not have a sweet tooth.

Sweets and fruit glazed with caramel also have a place among petits fours. In this section, the emphasis is on confections made with fresh and dried fruit and nuts, sparingly coated with caramel and chocolate.

Most of the recipes are simple. However, melting chocolate and making caramel require a little care and attention. When you are melting chocolate, choose a bowl that fits the saucepan exactly to prevent water from splashing into the chocolate; even one drop can turn it grainy. And never apply too much heat, since this causes white spots of cocoa butter to develop as the chocolate sets.

Before you start to make caramel, assemble all the ingredients and equipment, because once the syrup is ready you will have to apply it speedily before it starts to harden. To reduce the risk of the syrup's crystalliz-ing, ensure that every grain of sugar is dissolved before the syrup is brought to a boil, and stop stirring as soon as it comes to a boil. Humidity prevents caramel from hardening and makes it sticky, so avoid making car-amel on damp days or in a steamy kitchen, if possible.

Iced Sponge Cakes

Makes 30 cakes
Working time: about 1 hour and 25 minutes
Total time: about 1 hour and 40 minutes

Per cake:	
Calories **95**	3 eggs
Protein **1g.**	7 tbsp. sugar
Cholesterol **25mg.**	¾ cup unbleached all-purpose flour
Total fat **3g.**	2 tsp. strong black coffee, cooled
Saturated fat **1g.**	½ tsp. pure almond extract
Sodium **10mg.**	1 tsp. cocoa powder, sifted
	1 tbsp. finely shredded unsweetened coconut

Icings and toppings
3½ oz. semisweet chocolate, broken into pieces
3 crystallized violets, coarsely chopped
½ oz. hazelnuts, toasted and peeled (technique, page 29), chopped (about 2 tbsp.)
1¾ cups confectioners' sugar
1 tbsp. unsalted butter, melted
1 tsp. fresh lemon juice
½ orange, grated zest and 1 tsp. juice only
2 tsp. strong black coffee, cooled
3 tbsp. sliced almonds, toasted
½ candied orange or other candied fruit, finely sliced
½ oz. semisweet chocolate scrolls (technique, page 12)

Preheat the oven to 350° F. Lightly grease and flour 30 shallow tartlet molds of assorted shapes, each about 3 inches in diameter.

Place the eggs and sugar in a mixing bowl set over a pan of hot but not boiling water on low heat. Using an electric hand-held mixer, beat the eggs and sugar together until the mixture is thick and pale. Remove the bowl from the heat, and continue beating until the mixture is cool and falls from the beater in a ribbon. Sift the flour lightly over the surface of the mixture, then fold it in gently.

Divide the mixture equally among five small bowls. Leave one plain, and flavor each of the others by stirring in one of the four flavorings: coffee, almond extract, cocoa powder, and shredded coconut. Spoon the sponge mixtures evenly into the prepared molds and bake until they are golden—10 to 15 minutes. Gently unmold them and let them cool on a wire rack.

To ice the plain and coffee-flavored cakes with chocolate icing, put the chocolate into a bowl with 6 tablespoons of water; place the bowl over a saucepan of simmering water until the chocolate melts, then stir it. Allow it to cool until it thickens slightly—approximately five minutes. Place one of the cakes on a metal spatula, hold it over the bowl, and spoon the chocolate over it. Place the iced cake on a sheet of wax paper. Ice the remaining plain and coffee-flavored cakes in the same way. Decorate each plain cake with a piece of crystallized violet, sprinkle chopped hazelnuts over the coffee-flavored cakes, and let them set.

To ice the remaining sponge cakes, mix the confectioners' sugar with the melted butter and 3 tablespoons of warm water. Divide this mixture into three equal parts: Flavor one with the lemon juice, one with the grated orange zest and orange juice, and the third with the coffee. Using the same technique as for the chocolate icing, cover the almond cakes with lemon icing, the coconut cakes with orange icing, and the chocolate cakes with coffee icing. Decorate the cakes with sliced almonds, candied fruit, and chocolate scrolls respectively.

EDITOR'S NOTE: *To toast sliced almonds, put them under the broiler until they are golden—about two minutes—shaking them constantly.*

Fruited Turkish Coffee Squares

Makes 64 squares
Working time: about 30 minutes
Total time: about 1 hour and 30 minutes

Per square:
Calories **35**
Protein **1g.**
Cholesterol **5mg.**
Total fat **1g.**
Saturated fat **0g.**
Sodium **25mg.**

2 cups unbleached all-purpose flour
1 tsp. ground cinnamon
½ tsp. ground coriander
1 tbsp. coffee beans, very finely ground
7 tbsp. dark brown sugar
7 tbsp. polyunsaturated margarine
1 egg, beaten
2 large bananas, peeled and very thinly sliced lengthwise
3 fresh apricots (about 6 oz.), pitted and very thinly sliced
½ tsp. baking soda
½ tsp. baking powder
¾ cup plain low-fat yogurt
1 tbsp. confectioners' sugar

Preheat the oven to 400° F.

Sift the flour, cinnamon, coriander, and coffee together in a mixing bowl. Add the brown sugar and rub in the margarine until fine crumbs are formed. Divide the mixture into two portions in separate bowls. Add half the beaten egg to one portion, and mix with your hands to make larger crumbs and a slightly sticky consistency. Press this mixture firmly into the bottom of a pan that is 8 by 8 inches and at least 1½ inches deep. Arrange the banana slices in rows over the crumb base, and lay rows of apricot slices on top.

Stir the baking soda into the remaining fine crumb mixture; blend the baking powder with the remaining egg, and add this and the yogurt to the crumbs. Mix well with a wooden spoon until the mixture is smooth, then pour it over the fruit in the pan, making sure that the fruit is completely covered. Bake the cake until it is firm to the touch—30 to 40 minutes. Remove the cake from the oven and let it cool in the pan.

When the cake is cool, sift the confectioners' sugar over it and cut into 1-inch squares to serve.

EDITOR'S NOTE: *To give the squares a crunchier top, sprinkle a tablespoon of granulated sugar over the mixture before it is baked, and omit the confectioners' sugar. The squares may be stored in the refrigerator for two days.*

Candied Fruitcake Squares

Makes 64 squares
Working time: about 1 hour
Total time: about 5 hours and 30 minutes (includes drying)

Per square:
Calories **50**
Protein **trace**
Cholesterol **10mg.**
Total fat **1g.**
Saturated fat **trace**
Sodium **15mg.**

1 large thick-skinned grapefruit, peel only
¾ cup light brown sugar
½ cup pitted dates, cut into ½-inch pieces
⅓ cup candied red cherries, halved
¼ cup candied green figs, or dried figs, cut into strips
¾ cup walnuts, coarsely chopped
¾ cup raisins
3 eggs, beaten
½ cup dark brown sugar
1 tsp. pure vanilla extract
1 lemon, grated zest only
1 cup unbleached all-purpose flour
1 tsp. baking powder
1 tsp. ground cinnamon
½ tsp. pumpkin pie spice
3 tbsp. brandy or whiskey
½ cup apricot jam

Place the grapefruit peel in a saucepan, cover with cold water, and bring slowly to a boil, then drain thoroughly. Repeat this process three more times to rid the peel of excess bitterness. Cover the peel with cold water once more, bring to a boil, and simmer gently until the peel is soft but not breaking up—20 to 30 minutes. Drain the peel, reserving the water.

Prepare a syrup in the saucepan by dissolving the light brown sugar in ½ cup of the reserved water over low heat. Add the peel and cook it for another 20 to 30 minutes, uncovered, until it is completely translucent. Remove the peel from the pan and leave it on a wire rack for a few hours, until it is dry to the touch and easy to handle. (Or dry it for an hour in the oven at its lowest setting.)

Preheat the oven to 325° F. Cut the dried peel into ½-inch pieces and place them in a large mixing bowl. Mix in the dates, cherries, figs, walnuts, and raisins. In another bowl, blend the beaten eggs with the dark brown sugar, vanilla, and lemon zest. Sift the flour with the baking powder, cinnamon, and pumpkin pie spice, and blend the ingredients thoroughly with the egg mixture. Add this to the fruit and stir well, ensuring that each piece of fruit is lightly covered with batter.

Line a shallow 10-inch-square baking pan with parchment paper. Pour the cake mixture into the lined pan, level the top of the mixture, and bake in the oven until the top of the cake is set—about one hour. Remove from the oven, prick the surface of the cake all over with a fork, and drizzle the brandy or whiskey over it. Let the cake cool in the pan for 15 minutes before transferring it to a wire rack to cool completely.

Slice the cake into 1¼-inch squares. Heat the apricot jam over low heat until it is liquid, then press it through a fine sieve. Brush the hot, sieved apricot glaze over and around each square of cake.

EDITOR'S NOTE: *Closely wrapped in foil, the cake may be left to soften and mature for two days before it is cut into squares, which will give a moister result. If you are serving the cake without forks, brushing only the tops of the squares with 3 tablespoons of apricot glaze will make them less sticky to handle. The fruitcake squares will keep for about four weeks in an airtight container.*

Chocolate Kisses

Makes 36 kisses
Working time: about 40 minutes
Total time: about 50 minutes

Per kiss:
Calories **65**
Protein **1g.**
Cholesterol **0mg.**
Total fat **2g.**
Saturated fat **1g.**
Sodium **5mg.**

2 oz. semisweet chocolate
4 oz. blanched almonds, toasted and finely ground (about 1 cup)
4 oz. hazelnuts, toasted and peeled (technique, page 29), and finely ground (about 1 cup)
¾ cup cornmeal
⅔ cup confectioners' sugar
7 tbsp. sugar
1 tbsp. honey
2 egg whites
5 tbsp. apricot jam without added sugar

Preheat the oven to 425° F. Line two large baking sheets with parchment paper.

Break the chocolate into pieces and melt it in a flameproof bowl set over a pan of simmering water. Place the almonds, hazelnuts, cornmeal, both kinds of sugar, and the honey in a mixing bowl. Pour the melted chocolate over the ingredients and stir the mixture thoroughly, then add the egg whites and stir again until a stiff batter is formed.

Spoon the mixture into a pastry bag fitted with a ¼-inch star tip. Pipe 72 rosettes, each about 1½ inches in diameter, onto the prepared baking sheets; leave at least 1 inch between rosettes.

Bake the rosettes until they are set—8 to 10 minutes—then transfer them to wire racks and let them cool. Just before serving, sandwich the rosettes together in pairs, using the jam as filling.

EDITOR'S NOTE: *To toast almonds, put them under a hot broiler until they are golden brown—two to three minutes; turn or shake them constantly.*

Candied Fruit Diamonds

THIS RECIPE IS REMINISCENT OF THE FAMOUS FLORENTINE SPECIALTY, BUT IT OMITS THE TRADITIONAL CHOCOLATE COATING AND USES SOUR CREAM INSTEAD OF WHIPPING CREAM IN THE MIXTURE.

Makes 30 diamonds
Working time: about 25 minutes
Total time: about 45 minutes

Per diamond:
Calories **70**
Protein **1g.**
Cholesterol **5mg.**
Total fat **4g.**
Saturated fat **1g.**
Sodium **10mg.**

3 tbsp. unsalted butter
6 tbsp. sour cream
6 tbsp. light brown sugar
¾ cup chopped almonds, plus ¼ cup sliced almonds
2 oz. candied cherries, quartered (about ⅓ cup)
1½ oz. candied oranges, chopped (about ¼ cup)
1½ oz. candied figs, chopped (about ¼ cup)
1½ oz. candied apricots (about ¼ cup)
1 oz. crystallized orange peel, finely chopped (about 3 tbsp.)
½ cup unbleached all-purpose flour, sifted

Preheat the oven to 350° F. Line the bottom of a 13-by-9-inch cake pan with parchment paper.

Heat the butter, sour cream, and sugar in a pan over medium-low heat until the butter melts and the sugar dissolves. Remove the pan from the heat, and stir in the almonds, candied fruit, crystallized orange peel, and flour. Using a metal spatula, spread the mixture evenly in the prepared pan, and bake until it is golden brown and firm to the touch—20 to 25 minutes.

Let the cooked mixture cool a little in the pan, then transfer it to a cutting board. Peel off the parchment paper and cut into small diamonds for serving.

EDITOR'S NOTE: *A different selection of candied fruit can be used in place of those listed above.*

Almond Cookies with Kumquat and Ginger

Makes 30 cookies
Working time: about 30 minutes
Total time: about 50 minutes

Per cookie:
Calories **60**
Protein **1g.**
Cholesterol **0mg.**
Total fat **4g.**
Saturated fat **1g.**
Sodium **5mg.**

1 cup sugar, plus 2 tsp. for the glaze
2 egg whites, lightly beaten
1¼ cups ground almonds
1 orange, finely grated zest and juice
¼ tsp. pure vanilla extract
5 kumquats, sliced and seeded
2 tsp. diced preserved stem ginger

Preheat the oven to 350° F. Line a baking sheet with parchment paper.

In a mixing bowl, combine the cup of sugar with the lightly beaten egg whites, ground almonds, orange zest, and vanilla extract, and mix until the ingredients form a soft paste. Transfer the mixture to a pastry bag fitted with a ¾-inch star tip, and pipe 30 small stars onto the parchment paper. Decorate the top of each star with one slice of kumquat and a little diced ginger. Bake the cookies until they are golden brown—approximately 20 minutes.

In the meantime, prepare the orange glaze. Put the orange juice and the 2 teaspoons of sugar into a small saucepan. Cook over medium-low heat, stirring until the sugar has dissolved, then increase the heat and boil the mixture rapidly until it becomes syrupy—three to four minutes.

While the cookies are still warm, brush the orange glaze over the kumquat and ginger. Allow to cool before serving.

Chocolate-Dipped
Horseshoes

Makes 30 horseshoes
Working time: about 30 minutes
Total time: about 1 hour

Per horseshoe:	
Calories **100**	8 tbsp. unsalted butter
Protein **1g.**	¾ cup confectioners' sugar, sifted
Cholesterol **25mg.**	2 egg yolks
Total fat **5g.**	1 tsp. pure vanilla extract
Saturated fat **3g.**	1½ cups unbleached all-purpose flour
Sodium **75mg.**	¾ cup cornmeal
	1½ oz. semisweet chocolate, broken into pieces
	1½ oz. white chocolate, broken into pieces

Preheat the oven to 325° F. Line two large baking sheets with parchment paper.

Beat the butter and sugar together in a mixing bowl until the mixture is light and fluffy. Beat in the egg yolks and vanilla extract, sift in the flour and the corn-meal, and continue beating until all the ingredients are thoroughly combined.

Take a small piece of the dough and roll it between your palms into a ½-inch-thick rope. Cut the rope into 4-inch lengths, then curve each piece into a horseshoe shape and place it on the parchment. Roll and shape the remaining dough in the same way, spacing the horseshoes well apart on the baking sheet to allow for spreading. There should be 30 horseshoes in all.

Bake the horseshoes until they are light brown—15 to 20 minutes—then transfer them to wire racks and let them cool.

Melt the semisweet and white chocolate in separate flameproof bowls set over pans of simmering water. Dip the ends of half of the horseshoes in the semisweet chocolate and the remaining horseshoes in the white chocolate. Place them on a rack over a parchment-lined tray and let the chocolate set before serving.

Ganache-Filled Macaroons

CLASSIC CHOCOLATE GANACHE IS A LIGHT WHISKED MIXTURE OF MELTED CHOCOLATE AND WHIPPING CREAM. THIS LOW-FAT VERSION USES SOUR CREAM INSTEAD OF WHIPPING CREAM AND NEEDS NO WHISKING.

Makes 16 macaroons
Working time: about 30 minutes
Total time: about 1 hour and 15 minutes

Per macaroon:
Calories **80**
Protein **2g.**
Cholesterol **trace**
Total fat **4g.**
Saturated fat **1g.**
Sodium **10mg.**

1 cup ground almonds
6 tbsp. sugar
2 egg whites
½ tsp. pure almond extract
1 oz. semisweet chocolate
1 tbsp. sour cream
1 tsp. confectioners' sugar

Preheat the oven to 350° F. Line one large or two small baking sheets with parchment paper.

Put the almonds and sugar into a mixing bowl, and mix well together. In a small bowl, lightly beat one egg white with the almond extract until frothy, then pour this into the ground-almond mixture. Combine to form a soft paste. Spoon the paste into a pastry bag fitted with a ⅝-inch plain tip. Pipe thirty-two 1-inch mounds of the almond mixture onto the lined baking sheets, spacing them ½ inch apart. Put the remaining egg white into a small bowl and beat it lightly with a

fork, just enough to break it up. Brush each mound of almond mixture with egg white, flattening any points as you do so.

Bake the macaroons until they are light brown—10 to 15 minutes. Remove them from the oven and let them cool on the baking sheet for one to two minutes, then remove them from the paper. Using a finger, press the flat side of each one to make a small indentation. Place the macaroons on a wire rack to cool.

To make the ganache, melt the chocolate in a flameproof bowl over a saucepan of simmering water. Remove the bowl from the heat and stir in the sour cream. Refrigerate until the ganache begins to thicken—5 to 10 minutes.

Sandwich pairs of macaroons together with the ganache and put them back on the wire rack. Leave them in a cool place until the filling sets firmly—approximately five minutes. Lightly sift confectioners' sugar over the macaroons and place them in small paper candy cups to serve.

EDITOR'S NOTE: *The filled macaroons will keep for five to six days stored in an airtight container.*

Fig and Orange Petits Fours

Makes 28 petits fours
Working time: about 40 minutes
Total time: about 1 hour

Per petit four:
Calories **45**
Protein **trace**
Cholesterol **trace**
Total fat **3g.**
Saturated fat **1g.**
Sodium **10mg.**

2 tbsp. unsalted butter
2 tbsp. polyunsaturated margarine
1 orange, finely grated zest only
1½ tbsp. honey
1 egg white
6 tbsp. ground almonds
¼ cup cornstarch, sifted
¼ cup unbleached all-purpose flour, sifted
1 oz. pitted dates, chopped (about 3 tbsp.)
2 oz. dried figs, chopped (about ⅓ cup)
1 oz. candied orange peel, chopped (about 3 tbsp.)
confectioners' sugar (optional)
candied fruit, dried fruit, and candied orange peel (optional)
pistachio nuts, peeled and chopped (optional)

Preheat the oven to 375° F. Very lightly butter 28 petits-fours molds; each mold should be approximately 1½ inches across.

Put the butter, margarine, orange zest, and honey into a mixing bowl, and beat well together until the mixture is light and fluffy. Gradually beat in the egg white, then fold in the almonds, cornstarch, flour, dates, figs, and chopped peel.

Fill the molds with the creamed mixture and level the tops with a table knife. Place the molds on a baking sheet. Bake until the petits fours are risen, lightly browned, and firm to the touch—5 to 10 minutes. Carefully unmold them onto a wire rack to cool.

Serve in paper candy cups, either plain or—as here—decorated with a little sifted confectioners' sugar, candied and dried fruit, candied peel, or chopped nuts as desired.

EDITOR'S NOTE: *To peel pistachio nuts, drop them into boiling water and simmer for one minute. Drain thoroughly, then wrap them in a towel and rub them vigorously until they have shed their skins.*

Apricot and Hazelnut Petits Fours

THIS RECIPE IS IDEAL FOR USING UP SPONGE-CAKE TRIMMINGS
THAT MAY BE LEFT OVER FROM SEVERAL OF THE
RECIPES IN CHAPTER 2.

Makes 24 petits fours
Working time: about 20 minutes
Total time: about 1 hour and 20 minutes
(includes chilling)

Per petit four:
Calories **35**
Protein **1g.**
Cholesterol **10mg.**
Total fat **2g.**
Saturated fat **0g.**
Sodium **20mg.**

4 oz. sponge cake (recipe, page 11)
2 oz. dried apricots, finely chopped (about ¼ cup)
1 oz. hazelnuts, toasted and peeled (technique, page 29), finely chopped or coarsely ground (about ¼ cup)
2 tbsp. orange-flavored liqueur
2 tbsp. apricot jam without added sugar
2 tsp. confectioners' sugar

Place the cake in a food processor or a blender, and process into crumbs; you should have about 1 cup. Alternatively, rub the cake through a wire sieve. Put the crumbs into a mixing bowl with the apricots, hazelnuts, liqueur, and jam, and mix well together.

Gather up the mixture in your hands and roll it out, using the palms of your hands, into a long, thin roll. Flatten the top and sides a little, then cut the roll into 24 equal slices. Lay the slices flat on a work surface and sift the confectioners' sugar over them.

Place each slice in a paper candy cup. Chill the petits fours for at least one hour before serving.

Chocolate-Apricot Petits Fours

Makes 40 petits fours
Working time: about 1 hour
Total time: about 2 hours (includes chilling)

Per petit four:
Calories **70**
Protein **1g.**
Cholesterol **15mg.**
Total fat **4g.**
Saturated fat **2g.**
Sodium **5mg.**

1¼ cups unbleached all-purpose flour
¼ cup confectioners' sugar
6 tbsp. unsalted butter, diced
2 egg yolks
1 cup ground almonds
¼ cup sugar
3 oz. dried apricots, chopped (about ⅓ cup)
1 tbsp. apricot-flavored liqueur
½ lightly beaten egg white
2 tbsp. apricot jam
1½ oz. semisweet chocolate, broken into pieces

Sift the flour and confectioners' sugar into a bowl, then rub in the butter until the mixture resembles fine breadcrumbs. Add the egg yolks and mix together with a wooden spoon to make a fairly stiff dough. Knead the dough lightly until smooth. Cover tightly with plastic wrap and refrigerate for 30 minutes. Lightly grease one large or two small baking sheets.

Roll out the chilled dough, on a lightly floured surface, to a thickness of about ⅛ inch. Prick the dough well all over with a fork. Using a 2¼-inch fluted cutter, stamp out rounds from the dough and place them on the prepared baking sheets. Reknead and reroll the trimmings, prick the dough again, then stamp out more rounds; continue until all the dough is used up—you should have approximately 40 rounds. Refrigerate the rounds for 30 minutes. Meanwhile, preheat the oven to 375° F.

Bake the rounds until they are lightly browned—10 to 12 minutes. Transfer the cookies from the baking sheet to a wire rack to cool.

Put the ground almonds, sugar, and chopped apricots into a bowl, and mix well together. Mix in the apricot liqueur and just enough egg white to make a stiff paste. On a surface very lightly sifted with confectioners' sugar, knead the apricot paste until smooth, then roll it out to about ⅛ inch thick. Using a 1¾-inch plain cutter, stamp out rounds from the apricot paste. Reknead and reroll the trimmings, and cut out more rounds, again continuing until all the paste is used up and you have about 40 rounds.

Bring the apricot jam to a boil, pass it through a fine sieve to remove any solids, then brush each cookie base very lightly with the jam glaze. Place a round of apricot paste on top of each cookie base, pressing it firmly in position. Lay the petits fours out in a single layer on wire racks.

Melt the chocolate in a small, flameproof bowl over a pan of simmering water. Fold a wax-paper or parchment-paper pastry bag *(technique, page 13),* and fill it with the melted chocolate. Fold the top of the bag down and cut off the tip. Decorate each petit four with fine chocolate piping *(technique, page 13).* Leave them in a cool place until set—10 to 15 minutes.

EDITOR'S NOTE: *The petits fours may be stored in an airtight container for three or four days.*

Pistachio and Almond Petits Fours

THESE PETITS FOURS MAKE A DELIGHTFUL AFTER-DINNER TREAT SERVED WITH COFFEE.

Makes 28 petits fours
Working time: about 30 minutes
Total time: about 45 minutes

Per petit four:
Calories **60**
Protein **1g.**
Cholesterol **10mg.**
Total fat **4g.**
Saturated fat **1g.**
Sodium **15mg.**

1 cup ground almonds
6 tbsp. sugar
¼ cup cornstarch
2 tbsp. polyunsaturated margarine, melted and cooled
1 tbsp. sour cream
1 egg, beaten
1 tbsp. kirsch or amaretto
1 oz. pistachio nuts, peeled and chopped (about ¼ cup)
1 tbsp. confectioners' sugar

Preheat the oven to 375° F. Have ready 28 double-thickness paper candy cups.

Mix together the almonds, sugar, and cornstarch in a mixing bowl. Make a well in the center, then pour in the margarine, sour cream, egg, and kirsch or amaretto. Blend the ingredients well, with a wooden spoon, until smooth.

Spoon the almond mixture into the candy cups, filling each one three-quarters full. Sprinkle the pistachio nuts evenly over the top of the mixture, then sift on the confectioners' sugar.

Place the petits fours on a baking sheet, and bake until risen, very lightly browned, and firm to the touch—12 to 15 minutes. Transfer the petits fours from the baking sheet to a wire rack to cool.

EDITOR'S NOTE: *These petits fours are best eaten on the day they are made, but they may be kept for two to three days if stored in an airtight container. To peel pistachio nuts, drop them into boiling water and simmer for one minute, drain thoroughly, then rub them briskly in a towel.*

Ginger Snaps with Kumquat and Ginger Mousse

Makes about 20 ginger snaps
Working time: about 1 hour and 15 minutes
Total time: about 2 hours and 30 minutes (includes chilling)

Per snap:
Calories **75**
Protein **2g.**
Cholesterol **10mg.**
Total fat **4g.**
Saturated fat **2g.**
Sodium **15mg.**

4 tbsp. unsalted butter
¼ cup light brown sugar
2 tbsp. dark corn syrup
½ cup unbleached all-purpose flour, sifted
1 tsp. fresh lemon juice
½ tsp. ground ginger
Kumquat and ginger mousse
6 oz. kumquats, stems removed
6 tbsp. fresh orange juice
1½ tsp. powdered gelatin
1-inch piece preserved stem ginger
2 tsp. syrup from preserved stem ginger
¾ cup plain low-fat yogurt

First, make the mousse. Purée the kumquats in a food processor or a blender with 4 tablespoons of the orange juice. Pass the purée through a fine sieve and discard the seeds. Put the remaining 2 tablespoons of orange juice into a small bowl, sprinkle on the gelatin, and allow it to soften for two minutes. Place the bowl over a pan of simmering water and stir until the gelatin has completely dissolved.

Return the kumquat purée to the food processor or blender, and add the preserved ginger, ginger syrup, and yogurt. Process until smooth. Add the dissolved gelatin and process for another 20 seconds. Transfer the mixture to a bowl and put it in the refrigerator to set—about one and a half hours.

Preheat the oven to 350° F. Grease two baking sheets, and line them with parchment paper. Heat the butter, sugar, and corn syrup in a small, heavy-bottomed pan over medium-low heat. When the butter has melted and the sugar has dissolved, remove the pan from the heat and stir in the flour. Mix well until smooth, then add the lemon juice and ground ginger.

Drop 4 level teaspoons of the mixture onto each baking sheet, spacing them well apart. Put one sheet in the oven, and bake until the snaps are bubbly and golden brown—about 10 minutes. Halfway through the baking period, put the other sheet in the oven. When the snaps on the first sheet are done, remove them from the oven and let them stand for about one minute to firm up slightly. Then lift the snaps from the parchment with a metal spatula and shape them into cornets around a metal cream-horn mold *(technique, right)*. Place the shaped snaps on a wire rack.

Wipe the parchment with paper towels, refill the sheet with 4 more teaspoonfuls of mixture, and return it to the oven. Remove the second sheet of cooked snaps from the oven. Let them rest briefly, then shape them as before. Continue to cook and shape the snaps in batches until all the mixture is used up. If the snaps start to harden before they are all shaped, return them to the oven for a few seconds to soften them again.

Finally, transfer the kumquat and ginger mousse to a pastry bag fitted with a ½-inch plain tip, and fill the snaps. Serve immediately; the snaps will hold the mixture for about an hour before becoming soft.

Chocolate Snaps

Makes 20 snaps
Working and (total time): about 1 hour and 15 minutes

Per snap:
Calories **60**
Protein **1g.**
Cholesterol **5mg.**
Total fat **5g.**
Saturated fat **3g.**
Sodium **5mg.**

4 tbsp. unsalted butter
¼ cup light brown sugar
2 tbsp. dark corn syrup
½ cup unbleached all-purpose flour, sifted
1 tsp. fresh lemon juice
½ tsp. ground cinnamon
5 oz. semisweet chocolate, broken into pieces

Preheat the oven to 350° F. Grease two baking sheets and line them with parchment paper.

Put the butter, sugar, and corn syrup into a small saucepan, and stir them over low heat. When the butter has melted and the sugar dissolved, remove the pan from the heat and stir in the flour. Mix until smooth, then stir in the lemon juice and cinnamon.

Drop 4 level teaspoons of the mixture onto each baking sheet, spacing them well apart to allow the snaps to spread. Put one sheet in the oven, and bake the snaps until they are bubbly and golden—about 10 minutes. Halfway through the baking period, put the other sheet in the oven. When the snaps on the first sheet are done, remove them from the oven and let them stand for a minute or so, to firm up slightly. Lift the snaps off the baking sheet with a metal spatula and roll them around the handle of a wooden spoon (technique, below). Place the shaped snaps on a wire rack.

Wipe the parchment with paper towels, refill the sheet with four more spoonfuls of snap mixture, and return it to the oven. Remove the second sheet of cooked snaps from the oven. Allow them to stand briefly, then shape them as before. Cook and shape

the remaining snap mixture in staggered batches, following the same procedure. If the snaps start to harden before they are all shaped, return them to the oven for a few seconds to soften them.

When all the snaps are cooked, shaped, and cooled, melt the chocolate in a flameproof bowl set over a saucepan of hot water. Dip the ends of the snaps in the chocolate, and let them set on parchment paper.

EDITOR'S NOTE: *The snaps can be stored for up to a week in an airtight container.*

Shaping Snaps

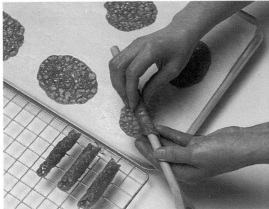

ROLLING CYLINDERS. Remove the snaps from the oven and leave them just long enough to be lifted without tearing—about one minute. Then lift one from the sheet with a metal spatula and quickly roll it around the handle of a wooden spoon. Slide the cylinder off the spoon handle as soon as it has set, and place it on a wire rack. Shape the remaining snaps in the same way.

MOLDING CORNETS. Remove the snaps from the oven and leave them just long enough to be lifted without tearing—about one minute. Then lift one from the sheet with a metal spatula and press it around a metal cream-horn mold to shape it into a cornet. Transfer the cornet to a wire rack as soon as it has set. Shape the remaining snaps in the same way.

Tulip Snaps with Amaretto Mousse

Makes 10 snaps
Working time: about 45 minutes
Total time: about 1 hour and 30 minutes (includes chilling)

Per snap:
Calories **110**
Protein **2g.**
Cholesterol **10mg.**
Total fat **7g.**
Saturated fat **3g.**
Sodium **10mg.**

2 tbsp. unsalted butter
2 tbsp. light brown sugar
1 tbsp. dark corn syrup
¼ cup unbleached all-purpose flour, sifted
½ tsp. fresh lemon juice
½ tsp. ground cinnamon
5 blanched almonds, split and toasted
Amaretto mousse
2 tsp. powdered gelatin
¾ cup plain low-fat yogurt
2 oz. amaretti cookies, crushed to a fine powder (about ⅔ cup)
1 tbsp. amaretto

First, make the mousse. Sprinkle the gelatin over 3 tablespoons of water in a small bowl. Allow it to soften for two minutes, then place the bowl over a saucepan of simmering water and stir until the gelatin has completely dissolved. In a separate bowl, mix together the yogurt, crushed amaretti cookies, and amaretto. Add the gelatin solution and stir the mixture thoroughly. Chill the mousse until it has set—about one hour.

In the meantime, make the tulip snaps. Preheat the oven to 350° F. Lightly grease two baking sheets and line them with parchment paper. Put the butter, sugar, and corn syrup into a small saucepan, and stir over low heat until the butter has melted and the sugar has dissolved. Remove the pan from the heat and stir in the flour. Mix until smooth, then stir in the lemon juice and cinnamon. Drop 4 level teaspoons of the snap mixture, spaced well apart, onto each of the baking sheets. Put one sheet in the oven, and bake the snaps until they are bubbly and golden brown—approximately 10 minutes. Halfway through the baking period, put the other sheet in the oven.

When the snaps on the first sheet are done, remove them from the oven, and let them stand for a minute or so to firm up slightly. Then lift them off the baking sheet with a metal spatula and drape them, topside down, over the bottoms of four upturned narrow glasses. The snaps will set in a tulip shape. Wipe the parchment lining with paper towels, refill the sheet with the last 2 teaspoonfuls of snap mixture, and return it to the oven. Remove the second sheet of cooked snaps from the oven. Let them rest briefly while you transfer the first batch to a wire rack, then shape the second batch in the same way. Finally, shape the remaining two snaps.

When the tulip snaps are firm, spoon the mousse into a pastry bag fitted with a ½-inch star tip, and pipe a rosette of the mixture into each tulip. Decorate the mousse with a half almond.

EDITOR'S NOTE: *To toast split almonds, put them under a hot broiler until they are golden—two to three minutes. Turn or shake them constantly.*

Nut-Filled Fruit

Makes 36 fruit
Working (and total) time: about 1 hour

Per fruit:
Calories **30**
Protein **1g.**
Cholesterol **0mg.**
Total fat **1g.**
Saturated fat **trace**
Sodium **5mg.**

12 fresh dates
12 small dried apricots
6 large pitted prunes
18 pistachio nuts, peeled and halved
1 tsp. confectioners' sugar
¾ cup sugar
Nut filling
¼ cup pistachio nuts, peeled and finely ground
¼ cup ground almonds
¼ cup confectioners' sugar
½ lightly beaten egg white

Begin by making the filling. Put the ground pistachio nuts, ground almonds, and confectioners' sugar into a mixing bowl, and mix well together with a wooden spoon; then add just enough egg white to bind the mixture into a stiff paste. Knead the mixture very lightly until it is smooth.

Very carefully slit each date lengthwise and remove the pit—do not cut the dates completely in half. Slit each apricot in half lengthwise—again, do not cut the fruit completely in half. Cut each pitted prune in half lengthwise, then smooth out each half to form the shape of a cup.

Divide the nut paste into 36 small pieces, and shape each piece into a neat oval shape by rolling it between your fingers. Fill the dates, prune halves, and apricots with the tiny ovals of nut paste, closing the fruit neatly around the sides of the filling. Decorate six of each type of filled fruit with a pistachio half, sift on the confectioners' sugar, place the fruit in paper candy cups, and set them aside.

Next, prepare a pan of caramel. Very lightly butter a baking sheet. Put the sugar into a heavy-bottomed saucepan with 3 tablespoons of cold water. Stir over low heat until every crystal of sugar has dissolved, brushing down any that stick to the sides of the pan with a natural-bristle pastry brush dipped in hot water. When the sugar has completely dissolved, bring the syrup to a boil, and boil it gently until it turns a very pale caramel color, or until the temperature on a sugar thermometer registers between 320° and 338° F. Immediately plunge the bottom of the saucepan into cold water to arrest the cooking and prevent the caramel from darkening any further. Then, to keep the caramel fluid, stand the pan in a bowl of very hot water.

Working very quickly, balance the remaining fruit, one at a time, on the end of a fork and dip them in the caramel. Allow the excess caramel to run back into the saucepan. Place the dipped fruit on the buttered baking sheet and decorate each one with a pistachio half; if the caramel begins to thicken, reheat it.

Leave the dipped fruit in a cool place until the caramel has set hard—5 to 10 minutes. Remove the fruit from the baking sheet and place them in paper candy cups. Arrange them, together with the sugar-coated fruit, on a serving dish.

EDITOR'S NOTE: *The caramel-dipped fruit may be stored in an airtight container, in a dry place, for one to two days. The sugar-coated fruit will keep for about two weeks. To peel pistachio nuts, blanch them in boiling water for one minute, drain them thoroughly, then rub them vigorously in a towel.*

Pecan-Chestnut Sweetmeats

Makes 25 sweetmeats
Working (and total) time: about 1 hour and 15 minutes

Per sweetmeat:
Calories **45**
Protein **trace**
Cholesterol **0mg.**
Total fat **1g.**
Saturated fat **trace**
Sodium **5mg.**

½ cup sugar
2½ tbsp. fresh orange juice
½ tsp. grated orange zest
3-inch piece cinnamon stick
50 pecan halves (about 2 oz.)
Chestnut purée
4 oz. chestnuts, peeled (technique, page 51)
2 tbsp. light brown sugar
1 tbsp. fresh orange juice
½ tsp. grated orange zest
¼ tsp. ground cinnamon
1 tbsp. brandy

Dissolve the sugar in the orange juice over low heat, add the orange zest and cinnamon, and bring to a boil. Continue to boil gently until a light caramel is produced, or until the temperature on a sugar thermometer registers between 320° and 338° F.—about 15 minutes. Remove the pan from the heat and place it briefly in a large pan of cold water to arrest the cooking process; then set it in hot water to keep the caramel fluid. Immediately coat the pecan halves in the caramel by spearing their flat sides with a skewer and dipping them into the syrup; as soon as each half is coated, use a lightly oiled fork to transfer the pecans from the skewer to parchment paper or a lightly oiled baking sheet. Let them harden.

To make the purée, put the chestnuts into a pan of boiling water, return the water to a boil, then lower the heat and simmer gently until the chestnuts begin to break apart—20 to 30 minutes. Drain them in a sieve or a colander. Prepare a syrup by boiling together the sugar and orange juice for two to three minutes. Process the chestnuts into a powder in a food processor or a blender, or press them through a fine sieve. Mix the chestnuts with the syrup, the orange zest, cinnamon, and brandy to obtain a creamy consistency.

Sandwich pairs of pecan halves together with a little of the chestnut purée and place them in paper candy cups. Serve while the nuts are still glossy—within a day of making them.

EDITOR'S NOTE: *The caramel may crystallize while the nuts are being dipped. If this happens, you will have to make another pan of caramel.*

Maple Sweetmeats

Makes 30 sweetmeats
Working time: about 30 minutes
Total time: about 1 hour and 30 minutes (includes chilling)

Per sweetmeat:	
Calories **35**	⅓ cup dried apricots
Protein **trace**	½ cup pitted fresh dates
Cholesterol **0mg.**	⅓ cup pitted prunes
Total fat **2g.**	6 tbsp. golden raisins
Saturated fat **1g.**	2 tbsp. maple syrup
Sodium **10mg.**	1 cup finely chopped unsweetened coconut
	2 tsp. cocoa powder

Put the apricots, dates, prunes, golden raisins, and maple syrup into a food processor, and blend until a sticky paste is formed. Transfer the mixture to a mixing bowl and add ¾ cup of the unsweetened coconut. Mix by hand to make a soft paste that is no longer sticky.

Divide the fruit paste into 30 equal pieces, then roll each one into a smooth ball. Place the remaining coconut in a dish and put the cocoa powder in another. Roll half of the balls in the coconut to coat them, then roll the remaining balls in the cocoa powder.

Place the sweetmeats in paper candy cups and refrigerate them for about one hour. Serve chilled.

EDITOR'S NOTE: *If you do not have a food processor, pass the fruit through the fine blade of a grinder; add the maple syrup with the coconut.*

Chocolate Rum Cups

Makes 12 cups
Working time: about 30 minutes
Total time: about 1 hour

Per cup:
Calories **105**
Protein **2g.**
Cholesterol **trace**
Total fat **5g.**
Saturated fat **3g.**
Sodium **5mg.**

2 oz. semisweet chocolate, broken into pieces
12 hazelnuts, toasted and peeled (technique, page 29)
Chocolate rum filling
4 oz. semisweet chocolate, broken into pieces
1 tbsp. dark rum
3 tbsp. plain low-fat yogurt

First, make the chocolate cups. Melt the 2 ounces of chocolate in a flameproof bowl set over a pan of simmering water until it is smooth but not runny; do not allow the chocolate to become too hot, or it will be very liquid and difficult to work with. Coat the insides of 12 double-thickness paper candy cups with melted chocolate as demonstrated at right. Chill the chocolate cups for about 30 minutes.

To make the filling, melt the chocolate in a flameproof bowl set over a pan of simmering water. Remove the bowl from the heat, stir in the rum and yogurt, and mix to form a smooth paste. Let the filling cool until it is firm, stirring it occasionally, then transfer it to a pastry bag fitted with a ½-inch star tip.

Carefully peel away the paper cups from the chocolate cups, and pipe a whirl of the filling into each chocolate cup. Place a hazelnut on top of each whirl.

Making Chocolate Cups

LINING CANDY CUPS. Melt chocolate in a flameproof bowl over simmering water until it is smooth but not yet runny. Spoon about ½ teaspoon into a foil or a double-thickness paper candy cup. Using a teaspoon handle, spread the chocolate evenly over the bottom and up the sides of the cup, then set the cup aside to firm up. When all the cups have been lined, chill them for 10 to 15 minutes, then repeat the process to add a second, thinner, layer of chocolate. Chill until firmly set—20 to 30 minutes.

Soft-Centered Chocolate Cups

Makes 30 cups
Working time: about 1 hour
Total time: about 1 hour and 30 minutes

Per cup:
Calories **35**
Protein **1g.**
Cholesterol **trace**
Total fat **2g.**
Saturated fat **1g.**
Sodium **10mg.**

5 oz. semisweet chocolate, broken into pieces
1 ripe peach, peeled and pitted
¼ cup fresh raspberries
2 tsp. powdered gelatin
⅔ cup sour cream
2 tbsp. confectioners' sugar
1 tbsp. Marsala
1 tbsp. kirsch
slivers of fresh fruit (cherries, oranges, grapes, kiwi fruit, raspberries, or peaches) to decorate

To make the chocolate cups, melt the chocolate in a flameproof bowl set over a pan of simmering water until it is smooth but not runny; do not allow the chocolate to become too hot, or it will be very liquid and difficult to work with. Coat the insides of 30 double-thickness paper candy cups with melted chocolate as demonstrated at left. Put the chocolate cups in the refrigerator to chill while you prepare the filling.

Purée the peach in a food processor or a blender, and then press the pulp through a fine sieve into a bowl. Press the raspberries through the fine sieve into a separate bowl; discard the seeds and reserve the raspberry purée.

Sprinkle the gelatin over 2 tablespoons of water in a flameproof bowl. Let it soften for two minutes, then place the bowl over a saucepan of simmering water and stir until the gelatin has completely dissolved.

Put half the sour cream into a bowl, and stir in the peach purée, 1 tablespoon of the confectioners' sugar, the Marsala, and half the gelatin solution. In a separate bowl, mix the rest of the sour cream with the raspberry purée, kirsch, and the remaining confectioners' sugar and gelatin solution.

Carefully peel away the paper cups from the chocolate cups. Using a teaspoon, fill half the chocolate cups with the peach filling and the other half with the raspberry filling. Decorate the filled cups with slivers of fresh fruit and chill them until the filling has set—at least 30 minutes. Serve the chocolate cups on the day they are filled.

EDITOR'S NOTE: *Unfilled, the chocolate cups may be stored in an airtight container in the refrigerator for several days.*

Chestnut Boats

Makes 20 boats
Working time: about 1 hour and 15 minutes
Total time: about 1 hour and 45 minutes

Per boat:
Calories **55**
Protein **1g.**
Cholesterol **0mg.**
Total fat **2g.**
Saturated fat **1g.**
Sodium **10mg.**

4 oz. semisweet chocolate, broken into pieces
6 oz. fresh chestnuts, peeled (technique, page 51)
1¼ cups skim milk
½ vanilla bean
1 tbsp. honey
3 tbsp. sour cream
½ tsp. pure vanilla extract
½ tsp. grated orange zest
1 orange, zest only, julienned, blanched for 1 minute, and drained

To make the boats, melt the chocolate in a flameproof bowl set over a pan of simmering water until it is smooth but not runny; do not allow the chocolate to become too hot, or it will be very liquid and difficult to work with. Follow the method for making chocolate cups *(technique, page 122)*, using 2-inch plain barquette molds instead of candy cups. Chill the boats in the refrigerator while you make the chestnut filling.

Put the peeled chestnuts into a small saucepan with the milk and vanilla bean; if necessary, add water to cover the chestnuts. Bring to a boil, then lower the heat and simmer gently until the chestnuts begin to break apart—20 to 30 minutes. Drain well, discarding the milk. (The vanilla bean may be rinsed, dried, and used again.) Process the chestnuts into a soft powder or press them through a fine sieve. Put the powdered chestnuts into a bowl, and stir in the honey, sour cream, vanilla extract, and grated orange zest to make a smooth cream. Spoon the mixture into a pastry bag fitted with a ¼-inch star tip.

Using a sharp knife, loosen and remove the chocolate boats from the molds. Pipe a little of the chestnut cream decoratively into each boat. Arrange strips of julienned zest over the chestnut cream. Serve the chocolate boats within two hours of filling them.

EDITOR'S NOTE: *The chocolate boats and the chestnut cream may be made a day or two in advance and stored separately in the refrigerator.*

Dried Fruit Nuggets

Makes 24 nuggets
Working time: about 45 minutes
Total time: about 4 hours

Per nugget:
Calories **65**
Protein **trace**
Cholesterol **0mg.**
Total fat **1g.**
Saturated fat **trace**
Sodium **10mg.**

¾ cup sugar
3-inch strip lemon zest
3-inch piece cinnamon stick
3 cloves
3 cardamom pods, lightly crushed
½ tsp. pumpkin pie spice
¼ cup dried apricots, cut into ¼-inch dice
¼ cup dried pears, cut into ¼-inch dice
¼ cup dried pineapple, cut into ¼-inch dice
¼ cup dried figs, cut into ¼-inch dice
2 tbsp. candied red cherries, quartered
2 oz. semisweet chocolate, broken into pieces

Dissolve the sugar in ½ cup of water in a medium-size, heavy-bottomed saucepan over low heat; brush down any sugar crystals that stick to the sides of the pan with a natural-bristle pastry brush dipped in hot water. Add the lemon zest, cinnamon, cloves, cardamom, and pumpkin pie spice, and simmer gently for five minutes. Remove the zest and whole spices with a slotted spoon, and discard them.

Increase the heat, place a candy thermometer in the pan, and bring the solution to a rapid boil. When the syrup reaches a temperature of 244° F., lower the heat, and add the diced apricots, pears, pineapple, and figs. Stir once, then cook the fruit for five minutes without stirring; the temperature should rise slightly during this period, but do not allow it to exceed 257° F. or the fruit may set too hard. Add the cherries and remove the pan from the heat.

Using a teaspoon and working quickly, lift spoonfuls of fruit out of the syrup and drop them in nuggets onto a sheet of parchment paper. Allow the fruit nuggets to cool at room temperature for at least three hours. When they are cool but still pliable, round them off with your fingers and put them on a fresh piece of parchment paper.

Melt the chocolate in a flameproof bowl set over a pan of simmering water. Fold a wax-paper or parchment-paper pastry bag *(technique, page 13)* and fill it with the chocolate. Fold down the top of the bag, cut off the tip, and drizzle zigzags of fine chocolate piping over the nuggets. Allow the chocolate to set for about 15 minutes before serving the nuggets.

EDITOR'S NOTE: *When the fruit mixture is spooned out into nuggets, the sugar syrup will tend to harden and crystallize; if it becomes too difficult to work with, reheat the mixture on low to melt the sugar again. The decorated nuggets may be stored in an airtight container for a few days, layered between sheets of parchment paper.*

Chocolate-Dipped Stuffed Prunes

THIS RECIPE PROVIDES AN IDEAL OPPORTUNITY TO USE UP SPONGE-CAKE TRIMMINGS THAT MAY BE LEFT OVER FROM SEVERAL OF THE RECIPES IN CHAPTER 2.

Makes 18 prunes
Working time: about 1 hour
Total time: about 3 hours

Per prune:
Calories **100**
Protein **1g.**
Cholesterol **0mg.**
Total fat **1g.**
Saturated fat **trace**
Sodium **20mg.**

½ cup sugar
6-inch piece cinnamon stick
1 vanilla bean
12 oz. large prunes (about 1½ cups)
2 oz. sponge cake (recipe, page 11)
2 oz. walnuts, lightly toasted and ground (about ½ cup)
4 tbsp. Armagnac or cognac
½ tsp. pure vanilla extract
2½ oz. white chocolate, broken into pieces

Place the sugar in a saucepan with 1 cup of water and heat on low until the sugar has dissolved. Add the cinnamon and vanilla bean, bring to a boil, then lower the heat and simmer for five minutes. Add the prunes and simmer for five minutes more. Using a slotted spoon, remove 18 large, well-shaped prunes and allow them to cool on a plate; then pit them carefully and open up the cavities for the filling. Meanwhile, continue simmering the remaining prunes until they are very tender—20 to 40 minutes—then transfer them to a plate to cool. Discard the syrup.

Next, make the filling. Pit the soft-cooked prunes, and place them in a food processor with the sponge cake, ground walnuts, Armagnac or cognac, and vanilla extract. Process until a smooth purée is formed. Using a teaspoon, press the filling into the prunes and bring the sides of each prune around the filling.

Melt the chocolate in a flameproof bowl set over a pan of simmering water until it is smooth and just free of lumps but still quite thick. Dip and turn each prune in the chocolate to coat one end. Arrange the prunes, filled-side up, on a sheet of parchment paper and set them aside until the chocolate has set. Serve them in paper candy cups.

EDITOR'S NOTE: *Stuffed prunes may be stored for several days in the refrigerator, layered between sheets of parchment paper in an airtight container. To toast walnuts, put them under a hot broiler until they begin to darken—about two minutes—stirring and shaking them constantly.*

Glazed Fruit

Makes about 45 glazed fruit
Working (and total) time: about 30 minutes

Per fruit:
Calories **15**
Protein **trace**
Cholesterol **0mg.**
Total fat **0g.**
Saturated fat **0g.**
Sodium **trace**

8 seedless red grapes
8 seedless green grapes
8 small strawberries, hulled
1 tangerine, peeled, segmented, all white pith removed from segments
6 raspberries
6 New Zealand gooseberries or pitted cherries
¾ cup sugar

Pierce each piece of fruit with a cocktail stick. Line a large baking sheet with parchment paper.

Place the sugar and 4 tablespoons of water in a small, heavy-bottomed saucepan. Set the pan over medium heat and stir the mixture gently with a wooden spoon to dissolve the sugar. Brush down any sugar crystals stuck to the sides of the pan with a natural-bristle pastry brush dipped in hot water. Warm a candy thermometer in hot water and place it in the pan. Bring the syrup to a boil and boil it rapidly until it reaches the soft-crack stage, when the temperature on the thermometer registers between 270° and 290° F. At this temperature, when a little syrup is dropped from a skewer into a bowl of ice water and then removed and stretched gently between the fingers, it will separate into strands that are hard but elastic.

Remove the syrup from the heat. Working quickly, dip the pieces of fruit, one at a time, into the sugar syrup, then set them on the prepared baking sheet to cool and harden. Allow the syrup to set for at least five minutes before you remove the cocktail sticks. Place each fruit in a decorative paper candy cup to serve.

EDITOR'S NOTE: *Prepare the fruit as near as possible to serving time, and keep them in a dry place. The sugar coating quickly becomes sticky in a damp or humid atmosphere.*

4 After expanding fivefold in only a few seconds, microwaved almond meringues (recipe, opposite) are sandwiched together with a light pastry cream.

Pastries from the Microwave

Efficient and versatile, a microwave oven can be an invaluable tool for making pastries. Its use need not be restricted to the recipes on the following pages, for though it is not suited to baking shortcrust or chou-puff doughs, it is ideal for preparing many individual elements of a recipe before final assembly. Many processes, such as melting chocolate and gelatin, are not only quicker in the microwave but also more convenient, since no saucepans are required.

When cooked in a microwave, a sponge mixture will rise to an amazing height in seconds without darkening in color, making it the perfect partner for pastel creams and mousses. Because of the speed of the process, follow the cooking times closely. The cake will be ready when it is springy to the touch, slightly shrunk away from the sides of the dish, and still a little moist on top. This moisture will evaporate if the sponge cake is left to stand, so do not be tempted to return it to the oven, or it will dry out.

Because microwave ovens do not burn food, pastry cream can be cooked until every trace of raw cornstarch has disappeared without fear of scorching the custard. Regular stirring with a wire whisk is all that is required to keep the custard smooth. Fruit cooked in a microwave retains its flavor and color. To preserve its shape, cook fruit in a single layer in a shallow dish, and to avoid moisture loss, cover the dish with plastic wrap made especially for use in the microwave. Always pull a corner of the plastic wrap back to prevent steam from building up.

Traditional meringues cannot be baked in a microwave oven, but the amaretto meringues here, with a large ratio of confectioners' sugar to egg white, have been specially created for this cooking method. A small amount of mixture—about ½ teaspoon—cooks to a large, fluffy meringue, so leave plenty of space around each one when baking them.

All the recipes in this section have been tested in 650-watt and 700-watt ovens. Although power settings may vary among different ovens, the recipes use "high" to indicate 100 percent power, "medium" for 50 percent power, and "medium low" or "defrost" for 30 percent power. The recipes also give instructions for turning the cakes so that they rise evenly, but these directions can be ignored if your microwave has an automatic turntable.

Amaretto Meringues

MICROWAVED MERINGUES ARE VERY DIFFERENT FROM THOSE COOKED IN A CONVENTIONAL OVEN: THEY ARE SOFT AND FRAGILE AND DISSOLVE IN THE MOUTH WHEN EATEN.

Makes 32 meringues
Working (and total) time: about 20 minutes

Per meringue:
Calories **65**
Protein **1g.**
Cholesterol **15mg.**
Total fat **2g.**
Saturated fat **trace**
Sodium **10mg.**

1 egg white
3½ cups confectioners' sugar
⅛ tsp. pure almond extract
⅓ cup slivered almonds
1 tbsp. amaretto
1¼ cups pastry cream (recipe, page 11 or 130)

Put the egg white into a bowl, sift in the confectioners' sugar, and add the almond extract. Stir the mixture until it is very stiff and firm; if it is sticky, add a little more confectioners' sugar—about 1 teaspoon.

Using your fingers, shape the mixture into 64 small balls of about ½ teaspoon each. Place eight balls, spaced well apart, in a circle on parchment paper. Using your thumb, lightly flatten each ball and press a few slivered almonds into the top of each. Microwave the balls on high for one minute, giving the paper a quarter turn every 20 seconds; the meringues will increase in size until they measure about 2½ inches, and they will hold their shape when cooked. If they collapse when the oven door is opened, cook them for 20 seconds more.

Remove the meringues from the oven, allow them to cool for one minute, then lift them off the paper and place them on a wire rack to finish cooling. Continue preparing and cooking the balls in batches of eight.

Stir the amaretto into the pastry cream. Using a small metal spatula or a table knife, spread about 1 tablespoon of pastry cream onto the flat surface of a meringue, then gently press the flat surface of a second meringue into the cream. Arrange the filled meringues on a serving plate and serve them immediately.

EDITOR'S NOTE: *The uncooked meringue mixture can be tightly covered with plastic wrap and stored in the refrigerator for up to three months. Cooked meringues can be stored in an airtight container for two weeks and filled with pastry cream as they are needed.*

Apple Castles

Makes 6 castles
Working time: about 30 minutes
Total time: about 1 hour and 30 minutes

Per castle:
Calories **160**
Protein **3g.**
Cholesterol **80mg.**
Total fat **2g.**
Saturated fat **trace**
Sodium **20mg.**

1 egg
¼ cup plus 3 tbsp. sugar
½ cup unbleached all-purpose flour
4 sweet apples
1 orange, juice only
6 tbsp. pastry cream (recipe, page 11 or box, below)
2 tbsp. orange-flavored liqueur
1 tsp. powdered gelatin
6 sprigs mint to decorate

Line the bottom of a 7-by-4-inch shallow baking dish with wax paper.

To make the cake, beat together the egg and ¼ cup of the sugar until the mixture is very thick and pale and falls from the whisk in a ribbon. Sift the flour over the surface of the beaten mixture, then fold it in gently with a large spoon. Pour the batter into the prepared dish, tipping the dish to distribute it evenly. Microwave on high until the sides of the cake begin to pull away from the dish but the top is still slightly moist—50 to 60 seconds. When the sponge cake is cool, turn it out onto a board and remove the paper.

Peel the apples, then core them, keeping them whole. With a sharp knife, cut the apples horizontally into thin, circular slices. Keep six small slices whole; cut the remainder in half. Put all the slices into a round, shallow dish, and sprinkle them with the remaining sugar and with the orange juice. Cover the dish with plastic wrap, leaving a corner open, and microwave on high until the slices are tender but still retain their shape—three to four minutes. Allow them to cool slightly. Drain the juices into a bowl and set aside.

Line the bottoms of six timbale molds with wax paper. Place a small whole apple slice in the bottom of each; if the slices will not fit, then cut them to size. Line the sides of each mold with the halved apple slices, using four or five slices per mold. Coarsely chop any remaining apple slices and stir them into the pastry cream with 1 tablespoon of the liqueur.

Sprinkle the gelatin over the reserved apple juices and let the mixture stand for two minutes. Microwave the mixture on high until the gelatin has dissolved—about 30 seconds—then thoroughly blend it into the pastry cream. Divide the mixture among the six molds.

Cut six disks out of the cake to fit snugly inside the apple slices, on top of the pastry cream. Sprinkle the remaining liqueur over the sponge-cake disks. Chill the molds for one hour, then unmold them and remove the paper. Serve decorated with a mint sprig.

Microwave Pastry Cream

Makes about 1¼ cups
Working time: about 20 minutes
Total time: about 1 hour and 45 minutes (includes chilling)

2 egg yolks
2 tbsp. sugar
¼ cup unbleached all-purpose flour, sifted
1½ tbsp. cornstarch, sifted
1¼ cups skim milk
1 tsp. pure vanilla extract
2 tbsp. sour cream
1 egg white

Put the egg yolks and half the sugar into a mixing bowl. Beat them together until the mixture is thick, then carefully fold in the flour and cornstarch. Gradually beat in the milk and vanilla extract to form a smooth batter. Microwave on high for three to three and a half minutes, beating every minute; when the mixture is cooked, it should form a thick, smooth custard. Cover the surface of the custard closely with plastic wrap to prevent a skin from forming. Allow the custard to cool for about 10 minutes, then refrigerate until it is almost cold—15 to 20 minutes.

Beat the custard until it is smooth, then whip in the sour cream. Beat the egg white until it is stiff, then whip in the remaining sugar until the mixture is shiny. Gradually fold the egg white into the custard using a rubber spatula. Cover the pastry cream with plastic wrap and chill it for at least one hour.

EDITOR'S NOTE: *The pastry cream may be stored in the refrigerator for up to two days.*

Banana Diamonds

Makes 12 diamonds
Working time: about 40 minutes
Total time: about 1 hour and 15 minutes

Per diamond:
Calories **190**
Protein **4g.**
Cholesterol **20mg.**
Total fat **6g.**
Saturated fat **1g.**
Sodium **180mg.**

1½ cups whole-wheat flour
½ tsp. baking soda
½ cup light brown sugar
4 tbsp. skim milk
2 ripe bananas, mashed
4 tbsp. safflower or sunflower oil
1 egg
½ tsp. baking powder
½ tsp. pure vanilla extract
2 tbsp. confectioners' sugar to decorate
Cheese filling
7 oz. low-fat cream cheese
3 tbsp. confectioners' sugar
3½ tbsp. fresh orange juice
1 tsp. pumpkin pie spice

Line the bottom of an 11-by-7-inch rectangular dish with parchment paper.

Sift the flour and baking soda into a large bowl, mix in the light brown sugar, then add the milk, bananas, oil, egg, baking powder, and vanilla extract. Beat the mixture until it is smooth, then transfer it to the lined dish; microwave on medium for six minutes, giving the dish a half-turn every two minutes. Increase the power to high, and microwave until the cake is springy to the touch but still moist—four to five minutes. Remove the cake from the oven and leave it in the dish for three minutes before inverting it onto a wire rack. Remove the paper and let the cake cool.

To make the filling, combine the cheese, sugar, orange juice, and pumpkin pie spice in a bowl.

Place the cake, right side up, on a work surface and trim around the edges to make a neat rectangle. Using a sharp, long-bladed knife, cut horizontally through the cake to make two equal layers. Spread the filling evenly over the bottom layer of the cake. Replace the top layer and cut the cake lengthwise into three equal strips. Cut each strip diagonally into four diamond shapes. (There will be two small triangles left over from the ends of each strip.)

Using stiff paper, cut out a diamond-shaped template the size of one of the banana diamonds. With a pencil, draw a large *X* across the middle, making four small diamonds. Cut out two facing diamonds, taking care to leave the other two joined in the center. Place the template on one of the banana diamonds and sprinkle it with the confectioners' sugar. Remove the template and repeat with the rest of the cakes.

Chocolate Boxes

Makes 18 boxes
Working time: about 1 hour
Total time: about 1 hour and 30 minutes

Per box:
Calories **70**
Protein **2g.**
Cholesterol **40mg.**
Total fat **3g.**
Saturated fat **1g.**
Sodium **20mg.**

1 egg
3 tbsp. sugar
⅓ cup unbleached all-purpose flour
2 oz. semisweet chocolate
1 tbsp. kirsch
1¼ cups pastry cream (recipe, page 11 or 130)
5 strawberries, hulled and quartered lengthwise

Line the bottom of an 8-by-4-inch loaf pan with wax paper. Put the egg and sugar into a mixing bowl, and beat until the mixture is very thick and pale and falls from the whisk in a ribbon. Sift the flour lightly over the beaten mixture, then fold it in gently with a rubber spatula. Pour the batter into the prepared dish, tipping the dish to distribute it evenly. Microwave on high until the sides of the cake begin to pull away from the dish, but the top is still slightly moist—about 50 seconds. Set the cake aside to cool in the dish.

Meanwhile, start making the chocolate squares. To mold the chocolate, you will need to fold a double thickness of aluminum foil to make a 12-by-6-inch "pan" with 1-inch sides. Set the pan on a baking sheet. Grease the pan and line it with wax paper. Break the chocolate into pieces and place them in a small bowl. Microwave on medium until the chocolate has melted—two and a half to three minutes—then pour it into the prepared pan, spread evenly with a metal spatula, and let it set in a cool place—about 30 minutes.

Invert the cooled cake onto a board and remove the paper. Using a sharp knife, trim all four sides to obtain neat straight edges. Then cut the sponge rectangle into 18 squares slightly smaller than 1 inch, and save the excess for another recipe. Cut the chocolate into 72 squares measuring 1 inch *(technique, page 12)*.

Stir the kirsch into the pastry cream. Using a small metal spatula or a table knife, spread a little of the pastry cream on the sides of the cakes and press a chocolate square to each side. Transfer the remaining pastry cream to a pastry bag fitted with a medium star tip. Pipe two lines of cream across each box and place a strawberry quarter on top.

EDITOR'S NOTE: *These boxes may be stored in the refrigerator for four or five days; do not top with fruit until serving time. The strawberries can be replaced by other fresh seasonal fruit, such as cherries, raspberries, tangerine segments, or kiwifruit slices, or by a colorful combination of several.*

Peach and Passionfruit Petits Fours

Makes 36 petits fours
Working time: about 1 hour
Total time: about 3 hours

Per petit four:
Calories **25**
Protein **2g.**
Cholesterol **15mg.**
Total fat **1g.**
Saturated fat **trace**
Sodium **25mg.**

1 tbsp. unsalted butter
2 eggs
¼ cup sugar
½ cup unbleached all-purpose flour
¼ tsp. baking powder
½ tbsp. fresh lemon juice
2 tbsp. raspberry jam without added sugar, sieved, to decorate
2-inch stick angelica, sliced diagonally into diamond shapes, to decorate (optional)

Peach filling

2 peaches, blanched for 30 seconds, peeled, pitted, thinly sliced, and covered with acidulated water
3 tbsp. confectioners' sugar
1 tsp. arrowroot
1 tbsp. fresh lemon juice
1½ tbsp. powdered gelatin
⅓ cup plain low-fat yogurt

Passionfruit icing

4 passionfruit
1 cup confectioners' sugar, sifted

Line the bottom of an 8-inch-square dish, at least 1½ inches deep, with parchment paper.

Place the butter in a small bowl, and microwave on low until it is melted—about one minute. Set aside to cool. Put the eggs and sugar into a mixing bowl, and beat until the mixture is very thick and pale and falls from the whisk in a ribbon. Sift the flour and baking powder lightly over the beaten mixture, fold them in gently using a rubber spatula, then carefully fold in the lemon juice and ½ tablespoon of water. Pour in the cooled butter, and fold it in quickly and thoroughly.

Pour the batter into the prepared dish, and microwave on high until the sponge cake is well risen and the surface still appears moist—two and a half to three minutes; give the dish a quarter turn every 45 seconds. Remove the cake from the oven and allow it to rest until no damp patches remain on its surface—five to eight minutes. Unmold the sponge cake onto a wire rack covered with a layer of wax paper, and let it cool.

To make the filling, dry the peach slices on paper towels, then place them in a bowl. Sprinkle the sugar over them, and microwave on high for one minute. Press the fruit through a fine sieve into another bowl. Dissolve the arrowroot in the lemon juice and stir this into the peach purée. Microwave on medium, stirring frequently, until the purée is thick and clear—about one minute. Remove the bowl from the oven and cool to room temperature—about 20 minutes.

Meanwhile, sprinkle the gelatin over 3 tablespoons of water in a small bowl. Let it soften for two minutes, then microwave on high until the gelatin has dissolved—about 30 seconds. Microwave the yogurt on low for one minute to bring it to room temperature. Beat the yogurt briefly until it is smooth, beat in the peach purée, then whisk in the gelatin. Place the filling in the refrigerator for 10 to 15 minutes to thicken.

Remove the parchment paper from the sponge cake and invert the cake onto a board. Using a sharp, long-bladed knife, cut the cake horizontally into three layers. Spread half the peach filling over the bottom layer. Set the middle layer of cake on the filling, cover that with the remaining peach mixture, and place the third sponge layer on top. Trim the edges with a sharp knife.

To make the icing, cut the passionfruit in half, and using a teaspoon, scoop the seeds and pulp into a fine sieve set over a bowl. Press the pulp through the sieve, then discard the seeds. Blend the sugar into the juice, adding a little water if necessary to achieve a thick coating consistency. Spread the icing over the top layer of cake with a metal spatula, then lightly score the top with the tip of a sharp knife to mark out 36 squares. Set aside until the icing has set—about one hour.

Fold a wax-paper or parchment-paper pastry bag (technique, page 13) and fill it with the jam. Decorate each square with the jam and angelica, if you wish. Cut the cake into the marked squares just before serving.

EDITOR'S NOTE: If you prefer, the uncut assembly may be covered with plastic wrap and stored in the refrigerator for four or five days. It can then be cut and decorated as desired.

Chocolate and Ginger Cheesecakes

Makes 6 cheesecakes
Working time: about 30 minutes
Total time: about 3 hours (includes chilling)

Per cheesecake:
Calories **210**
Protein **10g.**
Cholesterol **10mg.**
Total fat **9g.**
Saturated fat **5g.**
Sodium **230mg.**

3 whole graham crackers
2½ oz. semisweet chocolate
2 tsp. powdered gelatin
2 tbsp. honey
1 oz. crystallized ginger
1 cup plain low-fat yogurt
¼ cup half-and-half
1 tsp. confectioners' sugar to decorate

Cut six circles of wax paper to line the bottoms of six ½-cup ramekins, using a ramekin as a guide. Break the graham crackers into pieces, place them in a food processor, and process briefly to produce crumbs. Break 1½ ounces of the semisweet chocolate into a dish, and microwave on medium until the chocolate is melted—two and a half to three minutes. Stir until smooth, then combine with the graham-cracker crumbs. Divide the chocolate-crumb mixture among the ramekins, lightly pressing it into the bottoms. Chill until firm—about 20 minutes.

Sprinkle the gelatin over 2 tablespoons of water in a bowl and allow it to soften for two minutes. Microwave on high for 30 seconds to melt the gelatin. Stir in the honey and cool slightly.

Meanwhile, finely chop the ginger in a food processor, and combine it with the yogurt and half-and-half. Mix together until smooth, then blend in the gelatin mixture thoroughly. Divide the mixture among the ramekins, cover with plastic wrap, and chill for at least two hours, or preferably overnight, to set.

To make the topping, break the remaining chocolate into a dish, and microwave on medium for two to two and a half minutes. Stir the chocolate until it is smooth, then, using a metal spatula, spread it out in a very thin layer on a marble slab or an inverted baking sheet. Let it cool until it is almost set—three to four minutes. Push a pastry scraper under the chocolate to produce scrolls (*technique, page 12*).

Just before serving, slip a knife around the sides of the ramekins. Unmold each cheesecake first into the palm of your hand, to remove the lining paper, then place it on a board. Cover the cakes with chocolate scrolls. Sift confectioners' sugar over one half of the top of each one, using a spatula to cover the other half.

Pear and Hazelnut Galettes

Makes 8 galettes
Working time: about 30 minutes
Total time: about 1 hour

Per galette:	
Calories **175**	2 Bosc pears
Protein **2g.**	½ cup plus 2 tbsp. port
Cholesterol **30mg.**	⅓ cup sugar
Total fat **5g.**	1 tbsp. finely chopped crystallized ginger
Saturated fat **2g.**	6 tbsp. pastry cream (recipe, page 11 or 130)
Sodium **15mg.**	**Hazelnut shortbread**
	2 tbsp. unsalted butter
	1 tbsp. sugar
	6 tbsp. unbleached all-purpose flour
	2 tbsp. hazelnuts, toasted and peeled (technique, page 29) and finely ground

Peel the pears, cut them in half lengthwise, scoop out the cores, then cut the pears into long thin slices.

Combine the port and sugar in an 8-inch round dish. Microwave on high for two minutes, then stir until the sugar has dissolved. Place the pear slices in the syrup, turning them so that they are well coated. Cover the dish with plastic wrap, leaving a corner open. Cook the pears on high, giving the dish a quarter turn after three minutes, until they are tender but still hold their shape—six to eight minutes. At the end of the cooking time, loosen the plastic wrap and drain the juices into a flameproof bowl. Let the pears cool.

Heat the syrup on high, without stirring, until it has become quite thick and smells slightly of caramel—about seven minutes—then set it aside to cool.

Meanwhile, make the shortbread. Cream together the butter and sugar, then mix in the flour and hazelnuts to make a stiff dough. Turn the dough onto a lightly floured work surface and roll it out to a thickness of about ⅛ inch. Using a 3-inch plain cutter, cut out eight circles. Place a sheet of parchment paper in the microwave. Put four shortbread circles on the paper, and cook them on high for two minutes. Allow them to cool slightly before placing them on a wire rack and cooking the second batch.

Stir the chopped ginger into the pastry cream. Spoon a little cream onto the eight cooled shortbread circles, spreading it to within ¼ inch of the edges. Arrange three or four pear slices on each shortbread base, trimming the fruit to size if necessary. Place the galettes on a wire rack set over a baking sheet and drizzle the syrup over the pears. Serve immediately.

Chocolate Bombes

Makes 12 bombes
Working time: about 45 minutes
Total time: about 3 hours (includes chilling)

Per bombe:
Calories **150**
Protein **5g.**
Cholesterol **15mg.**
Total fat **9g.**
Saturated fat **5g.**
Sodium **140mg.**

1 cup low-fat cottage cheese	
2 tbsp. sugar	
4 tbsp. whipping cream	
½ lemon, grated zest only	
1 oz. candied cherries, finely chopped (about 2 tbsp.)	
1 oz. candied ginger, finely chopped (about 2 tbsp.)	
1 tbsp. coffee-flavored liqueur	
1 oz. walnuts, finely chopped (about ¼ cup)	
1-inch cube crystallized ginger, chopped, to decorate	
Chocolate coating	
3 oz. semisweet chocolate	
3 tbsp. unsalted butter	

Sieve the cottage cheese into a bowl, add the sugar and cream, and beat with an electric mixer until the mixture is very light. Divide the mixture evenly between two bowls. Add the lemon zest, cherries, and ginger to one bowl. Stir the coffee-flavored liqueur and walnuts into the other bowl. Set both bowls aside.

Use plastic egg cartons as molds for the bombes. Line 12 molds with pieces of plastic wrap. Distribute the fruit and cottage cheese mixture evenly among the molds, smooth the surfaces, then spoon on the nut mixture and smooth the tops again. Chill the bombes for two hours.

To make the coating, put the chocolate and butter into a small bowl, and microwave on medium until both the chocolate and butter have melted—three to four minutes. Stir the mixture until it is smooth, then let it cool until it just begins to set.

Unmold the bombes onto a board and remove the plastic wrap. Slide a metal spatula under one bombe, hold it over the bowl of melted chocolate, and carefully spoon the mixture over the bombe, spreading it with a knife to ensure an even coating. Set the bombe on a wire rack and score the surface with the tines of a fork. Coat the remaining bombes in the same way. Decorate each one with a piece of crystallized ginger.

Serve the bombes when the chocolate coating has completely set—10 to 15 minutes.

EDITOR'S NOTE: *The bombes may be stored in the refrigerator for up to four days.*

Candied Fruit Sticks

Makes 36 sticks
Working time: about 45 minutes
Total time: about 2 days and 2 hours
(includes 2 days' soaking)

Per stick:
Calories **51**
Protein **trace**
Cholesterol **0mg.**
Total fat **1g.**
Saturated fat **trace**
Sodium **2mg.**

1 lemon
1 orange
1 tsp. baking soda
1½ cups sugar
2 oz. milk chocolate
1½ oz. semisweet chocolate

Wash the lemon and orange thoroughly, slit through the peel with a sharp knife to divide it into quarters, then carefully remove the whole quarters of peel.

Place the baking soda in a bowl and stir in 2½ cups of boiling water. Immerse the peel, weight it down with a saucer, and let it soften for 20 minutes. Drain and rinse the peel, then cut it lengthwise into ¼-inch sticks. Place the sticks in a bowl with 2 cups of cold water. Cover the bowl with plastic wrap, leaving one corner open, and microwave on high, stirring once, until the peel is tender—approximately 25 minutes. Drain the cooked peel.

Combine 1 cup of the sugar with 1¼ cups of cold water in a 2-quart mixing bowl. (Do not use a smaller bowl, or the hot sugar syrup will boil over in the microwave.) Cook the mixture on high, stirring two or three times, until the sugar has completely dissolved—about eight minutes. Immerse the sticks of peel in the syrup, cover the bowl, and let them soak for two days.

Remove the sticks from the syrup with a slotted spoon and place them on a plate. Add the remaining sugar to the syrup, and microwave on high, stirring once, until the sugar has dissolved and the syrup is boiling—about six minutes. Return the sticks to the boiling syrup, and microwave them on high until they look translucent—10 to 13 minutes. Watch them carefully toward the end of the cooking time—they can easily burn in the hot syrup if left too long.

Place a sheet of parchment paper in the microwave. Drain the sticks well and spread them out in a single layer on the paper. Microwave on medium low for 24 minutes, moving the strips every six minutes to ensure even drying. The sticks are ready when they feel just dry and look sugary. Let them cool.

Break the milk chocolate into a bowl, and microwave it on medium until it is melted—two and a half to three minutes. Stir well until the chocolate is smooth, then hold an orange stick in your fingers and half dip it in the chocolate. Set the coated stick on a sheet of parchment paper. Continue until all the orange sticks have been dipped. Melt the semisweet chocolate and half dip the lemon sticks in the same way. Let the dipped sticks set for 10 minutes.

EDITOR'S NOTE: *The candied orange and lemon sticks can be left uncoated, and either eaten as a candy or chopped and used to flavor cookies and cakes. Store them in an airtight container for up to three months; once dipped in chocolate, the fruit sticks should be stored in the refrigerator for up to three weeks only.*

Glossary

Amaretto: an almond-flavored liqueur.
Angelica: the stalk of the angelica plant that has been candied in sugar syrup. Cut into delicate shapes, it is used as a decoration.
Armagnac: a dry brandy, often more strongly flavored than cognac, from the Armagnac district of southwest France.
Arrowroot: a tasteless, starchy white powder refined from the root of a tropical plant; it is used to thicken purées and sauces. Unlike flour, it is transparent when cooked.
Baking powder: a leavening agent that releases carbon dioxide during baking, causing cake batter or cookie dough to rise. Ordinary baking powders, as used in these recipes, have a high sodium content, but low-sodium baking powder is available for people on restricted-sodium diets.
Baking soda: a leavening agent in cakemaking, it is activated when combined with an acidic ingredient such as vinegar or molasses.
Calorie (kilocalorie): a unit of measurement used to gauge the amount of energy a food supplies when it is broken down for use in the body.
Calvados: an apple brandy made in the Normandy region of France.
Candied fruit: fruit—usually cherries, peaches, pears, plums, figs, apricots, or pineapple—preserved in sugar syrup, often used to decorate pastries or sweets.
Candy cups: small paper cases for holding sweets and petits fours. If they are to be used to bake petits fours in, the candy cups should be made of unwaxed paper.
Caramelize: to heat sugar, or a naturally sugar-rich food such as fruit, until the sugar turns brown and syrupy.
Cardamom: the bittersweet, aromatic dried seeds or whole pods of a plant in the ginger family. Cardamom seeds may be used whole or ground.
Chocolate: the refined product of the cocoa bean. For baking, select good-quality dark chocolate, which contains a high proportion—about 50 percent—of cocoa butter and cocoa solids and little or no vegetable fat.
Cholesterol: a waxlike substance that is manufactured in the human liver and also found in foods of animal origin. Although a certain amount of cholesterol is necessary for producing hormones and building cell walls, an excess can accumulate in the arteries, contributing to heart disease. See also Monounsaturated fat; Polyunsaturated fat; Saturated fat.
Cocoa powder: the result of pulverizing roasted cocoa beans, then removing most of the fat, or cocoa butter.
Confectioners' sugar (also called powdered sugar or 10X sugar—its most refined form): finely ground granulated sugar, with a small amount of added cornstarch to ensure a powdery consistency. The sugar's ability to dissolve instantly makes it ideal for desserts in which a grainy texture is undesirable.
Cornstarch: a starchy white powder made from corn kernels and used to thicken many puddings and sauces. Like arrowroot, it is transparent when cooked and makes a more efficient thickener than

flour. When cooked conventionally, a liquid containing cornstarch must be stirred constantly in the early stages to prevent lumps from forming.
Crystallized ginger (also called candied ginger): the spicy, rootlike stems of ginger preserved dry with sugar. Crystallized ginger should not be confused with ginger in syrup; the two are not always interchangeable.
Dates: the fruit of the date palm, dates can be bought fresh or dried. When dried dates are specified, choose plump unpitted dates in preference to pressed slab dates.
Dietary fiber: a plant-cell material that is undigested or only partially digested in the human body, but which promotes healthy digestion of other food matter. Also called roughage.
Eau de vie: a clear white liqueur distilled from fruit such as pears or raspberries.
Fat: a basic component of many foods, comprising three types of fatty acid—saturated, monounsaturated, and polyunsaturated—in varying proportions. See also Mononunsaturated fat; Polyunsaturated fat; Saturated fat.
Fiber: see Dietary fiber.
Gelatin: a virtually tasteless protein, available in powdered form or in sheets. Dissolved gelatin is used to set mousses and fillings so that they retain their shape when unmolded.
Ginger: the spicy, rootlike stem of the ginger plant, used as a flavoring, either in fresh form, dried and powdered, or preserved whole in syrup. See also Crystallized ginger; Preserved stem ginger.
Glaze: to coat the surface of a tart or cake with a thin, shiny layer of melted jam or caramel.
Hazelnut (also called filbert): the fruit of a shrublike tree found primarily in Turkey, Italy, and Spain, and in the states of Washington and Oregon. Filberts, which are cultivated, have a stronger flavor than hazelnuts, which grow wild. Both are prized by bakers and candymakers.
Jam without added sugar: jam that is sweetened by the sugar naturally found in fruit (fructose), rather than by added sugar (sucrose). Once opened, it must be stored in the refrigerator, where it will keep for about three weeks. If jam without added sugar is unavailable, use a low-sugar jam.
Jelly-roll pan: a shallow rectangular baking pan, about 1 inch deep.
Kataifi: a Greek pastry made in long, thin strands like vermicelli. It can be bought ready-made from continental delicatessens and specialty shops.
Kirsch (also called kirschwasser): a clear cherry brandy distilled from small black cherries grown in Switzerland and Germany, as well as in the Alsace region of France.
Kiwi fruit: an egg-shaped fruit with a fuzzy brown skin, tart, lime-green flesh, and hundreds of tiny black edible seeds. Peeled and sliced horizontally, the kiwi displays a starburst of seeds at its center that lends a decorative note to toppings.
Kumquat: a small, oval orange fruit; both the skin and the flesh can be eaten.
Mace: the pulverized covering of the nutmeg seed, widely used as a flavoring agent in baking.
Mango: a fruit grown throughout the tropics, with

sweet, succulent, yellow-orange flesh that is extremely rich in vitamin A. Like papaya, it may cause an allergic reaction in some individuals.
Maple syrup: a sweet, golden syrup produced from the sap of the maple tree.
Marsala: a dark Sicilian dessert wine with a caramelized flavor.
Meringue: an airy concoction made from stiffly beaten egg whites and sugar. It can be baked to produce edible baskets, layered between sponge cake to make up a gâteau, or served on its own.
Mixed candied peel: the peel of citrus fruit, soaked in a concentrated sugar solution. It can be bought whole or already chopped.
Monounsaturated fat: one of the three types of fats found in foods. Mononunsaturated fats are believed not to raise the level of cholesterol in the blood. Some new evidence indicates that oils high in monounsaturated fats—olive oil, for example—may even lower the blood-cholesterol level.
New Zealand gooseberry or cape gooseberry: a small, tart fruit enclosed in a delicate papery husk. It can be eaten raw or cooked.
Nonreactive pan or bowl: a cooking vessel whose surface does not react chemically with the acids in food. Ovenproof clay, stainless steel, enamel, glass, and nonstick-coated aluminum are all considered nonreactive materials.
Parchment paper: a reusable paper treated with silicone to produce a nonstick surface. It is used to line pans and baking sheets, and to wrap food for baking.
Passionfruit: a juicy, fragrant, egg-shaped tropical fruit with wrinkled skin, yellow flesh, and many black seeds. The seeds are edible; the skin is not.
Persimmon: a soft fruit with a deep orange flesh.
Phyllo (also spelled "filo"): a paper-thin flour-and-water pastry used notably in Greek and Turkish cuisine. It can be made at home or bought, fresh or frozen, from delicatessens and shops specializing in Middle Eastern food. Because frozen phyllo dries out easily, it should be thawed in the refrigerator, and any phyllo sheets waiting to be filled should be covered with a damp towel.
Pine nuts (also called *pignoli*): seeds from the cones of the stone pine, a tree native to the Mediterranean. Toasting brings out their buttery flavor.
Pistachio nuts: prized for their pleasant flavor and green color, pistachio nuts must be shelled and boiled for a few minutes before their skins can be removed.
Poach: to cook a food in barely simmering liquid as a means of preserving moisture and adding flavor. Fruit may be poached in water, wine, or a light syrup.
Polyunsaturated fat: one of the three types of fats found in foods. It exists in abundance in such vegetable oils as safflower, sunflower, corn, and soybean. Polyunsaturated fats lower the level of cholesterol in the blood.
Pomegranate: a red-skinned fruit with succulent edible seeds that are picked out and eaten; the bitter white membranes are discarded. Pomegranates are in season in the autumn.

Poppy seeds: the spherical black seeds produced by a variety of poppy plant and used as an ingredient in pastries. Poppy seeds are so small that 1 pound numbers nearly a million seeds.

Port: a ruby-colored sweet dessert wine, originally from the Portuguese seaside town of Oporto, fortified with a small amount of brandy and usually aged in wooden casks.

Preserved stem ginger: pieces of peeled ginger root preserved in sugar syrup.

Purée: to reduce food to a smooth consistency by mashing it, passing it through a sieve, or processing it in a food processor or a blender.

Quince: a small, hard, green- or yellow-skinned fruit with a tart flavor. It cannot be eaten raw; the flesh turns pink when cooked.

Ramekin: a small, round, straight-sided glass or porcelain mold used to bake or serve a single portion of food.

Recommended Dietary Allowance (RDA): the average daily amount of an essential nutrient as recommended for healthy people of various ages by the National Research Council.

Reduce: to boil down a liquid in order to concentrate its flavor and thicken its consistency.

Ricotta cheese: a creamy, white Italian cheese made from whey. In the United States, it is made from whey and milk. One cup of part-skim ricotta cheese contains 19 grams of total fat.

Ring mold or savarin mold: a small, circular pan with a hollow center. Its open center nearly doubles the food surfaces that are exposed to its metal walls, thus speeding up the cooking time.

Rolled oats: a cereal made from oats that have been ground into meal, then steamed, rolled into flakes, and dried.

Rose water: a flavoring produced by distilling the oil of rose petals.

Safflower oil: the vegetable oil that contains the highest proportion of polyunsaturated fats.

Saffron: the dried yellowish red stigmas of the crocus flower, saffron yields a pungent flavor and a bright yellow color.

Saturated fat: one of the three types of fats found in foods. Found in abundance in animal products and coconut and palm oils, saturated fats raise the level of cholesterol in the blood. Because high blood-cholesterol levels contribute to heart disease, saturated-fat consumption should be kept to a minimum—preferably less than 10 percent of the calories consumed each day.

Savarin: a yeast-risen cake, soaked in sugar syrup and flavored with rum or brandy. The cake is named after Brillat-Savarin, an 18th-century writer on gastronomical subjects.

Semolina: a coarse meal made from wheat.

Simmer: to heat a liquid to just below the boiling point so that the liquid's surface barely ripples.

Skim milk: milk from which almost all the fat has been removed.

Sodium: a nutrient essential to maintaining the proper balance of fluids in the body. In most diets, a major source of the element is table salt, which contains 40 percent sodium. Excess sodium may contribute to high blood pressure, which increases the risk of heart disease. One teaspoon of salt, with 2,132 milligrams of sodium, contains about two-thirds of the maximum ''safe and adequate'' daily sodium intake recommended by the National Research Council.

Streusel: a coarse crumb topping, usually made by combining flour, butter, sugar, and flavorings.

Total fat: an individual's daily intake of poly-unsaturated, monounsaturated, and saturated fats. Nutritionists recommend that total fat constitute no more than 30 percent of the calories in the diet. The term as used in this book refers to the combined fats in a given dish or food.

Vanilla bean: the fermented and cured pod of a climbing orchid, native to Central America, used as a flavoring. The whole pod may be steeped in a liquid, or the pod may be split and the tiny black seeds inside scraped out and used.

Vanilla extract: pure vanilla extract is the flavoring obtained by macerating vanilla pods in an alcohol solution. Artificial vanilla flavoring is chemically synthesized from clove oil.

Vanilla sugar: sugar flavored by placing a whole vanilla pod in an airtight container of sugar for about a week.

Whole-wheat flour: wheat flour that contains the whole of the wheat grain with nothing added or taken away. It is nutritionally valuable as a source of dietary fiber, and it is higher in B vitamins than white flour.

Yeast: a microorganism that feeds on sugars and starches to produce carbon dioxide and thus leaven a cake or pastry. Yeast can be bought either fresh or dried; fresh yeast will keep for up to six weeks in a refrigerator.

Yogurt: A smooth-textured, semisolid cultured-milk product made with varying percentages of fat.

Zest: the flavorful outermost layer of citrus-fruit peel; it should be cut or grated free of the white pith that lies beneath it.

Index

Picture Credits

Credits from left to right are separated by semicolons, from top to bottom by dashes.

Cover: Martin Brigdale. 4: James Murphy—Graham Kirk; Simon Butcher. 5: James Murphy, except right by Chris Knaggs. 6: Chris Knaggs. 10, 11: Andrew Whittuck. 12: Ian O'Leary—John Elliott. 13: John Elliott, except bottom right by Ian O'Leary. 14, 15: Chris Knaggs. 16: James Murphy. 17: John Elliott. 18: Chris Knaggs. 19: Graham Kirk. 20, 21: Jan Baldwin. 22: Simon Butcher. 23: David Johnson—Chris Knaggs. 24: Martin Brigdale. 25: Graham Kirk. 26: Martin Brigdale. 27, 28: Chris Knaggs. 29: top, Graham Kirk—John Elliott. 30: Chris Knaggs. 31: Graham Kirk. 32: Chris Knaggs. 33: Graham Kirk. 34: Chris Knaggs. 35: James Murphy. 36-38: Chris Knaggs. 39: James Murphy. 40: Chris Knaggs. 41: Chris Knaggs—Jan Baldwin. 42: Simon Butcher. 43: Jan Baldwin. 44, 45: Martin Brigdale. 46: David Johnson. 47: James Murphy. 48: Chris Knaggs. 49: John Elliott. 50: James Murphy. 51: John Elliott. 52: Chris Knaggs. 53: Graham Kirk. 54: Simon Butcher. 55: Ian O'Leary. 56: Simon Butcher. 57: Chris Knaggs. 58: Graham Kirk. 59: John Elliott. 60: James Murphy. 61: Ian O'Leary. 62: Chris Knaggs. 63: James Murphy. 64, 65: Chris Knaggs. 66: Graham Kirk—John Elliott. 67: Graham Kirk. 68, 69: John Elliott. 70: Martin Brigdale—John Elliott. 71: John Elliott. 72: Jan Baldwin. 73: Simon Butcher. 74: James Murphy. 75, 76: Graham Kirk. 77: Ian O'Leary. 78: Jan Baldwin. 79, 80: James Murphy. 81: Martin Brigdale. 82: Simon Butcher. 83-85: James Murphy. 86: John Elliott. 87: John Elliott—Jan Baldwin. 88: Chris Knaggs. 89: Graham Kirk. 90: David Johnson. 91: John Elliott. 93: James Murphy. 94: John Elliott. 95, 96: James Murphy. 97: Ian O'Leary. 98: John Elliott. 99: Ian O'Leary. 100, 101: David Johnson. 102, 103: Chris Knaggs. 104: James Murphy. 105, 106: Jan Baldwin. 107: Chris Knaggs. 108: Martin Brigdale. 109: Simon Butcher. 110: Chris Knaggs. 111: David Johnson. 112: Chris Knaggs. 113: David Johnson. 114: Chris Knaggs.

115: Martin Brigdale. 116: Graham Kirk. 117: Martin Brigdale—John Elliott. 118: Jan Baldwin. 119: David Johnson. 120: Jan Baldwin. 121: Chris Knaggs. 122: Graham Kirk—John Elliott. 123: David Johnson. 124: Jan Baldwin. 125, 126: Martin Brigdale. 127: James Murphy. 128: Martin Brigdale. 130: Chris Knaggs. 131: Simon Butcher. 132: Jan Baldwin. 133: Martin Brigdale. 134: John Elliott. 135: Chris Knaggs. 136, 137: James Murphy.

Props: The Editors wish to thank the following outlets and manufacturers; all are based in London unless otherwise stated. 4: fork, Mappin & Webb Silversmiths—left, marble, W. E. Grant & Co. (Marble) Ltd.; right, napkins, Kilkenny. 5: left: china, Royal Worcester, Worcester; lace cloth, Laura Ashley Ltd. 17: plates, Inshop. 19: china, Fortnum & Mason. 22: fork, Mappin & Webb Silversmiths. 23: bottom: pottery, Winchcombe Pottery, The Craftsmen Potters Shop; marble, W. E. Grant & Co. (Marble) Ltd. 24: china, Fortnum & Mason. 27, 28: china, Villeroy & Boch. 29: top: marble, W. E. Grant & Co. (Marble) Ltd. 31: plate, The Conran Shop. 32: pottery, Kilkenny. 33: china, The Conran Shop. 34: china, Royal Worcester, Worcester; silver, Mappin & Webb Silversmiths. 37: marble, W. E. Grant & Co. (Marble) Ltd. 38: plate, Hutschenreuther (U.K.) Ltd.; marble, W. E. Grant & Co. (Marble) Ltd. 42: napkins, Kilkenny. 47: lace cloths, Laura Ashley Ltd. 50: fork, Mappin & Webb Silversmiths. 52: plates, Royal Worcester, Worcester. 54: plate, cup, and saucer, Chinacraft Ltd. 55: china, Royal Worcester, Worcester; lace cloth, Laura Ashley Ltd. 57: china, Hutschenreuther (U.K.) Ltd. 58: platter, Hutschenreuther (U.K.) Ltd. 59: plates, Royal Worcester, Worcester; forks, Mappin & Webb Silversmiths. 60: plate, A. & J. Young, The Craftsmen Potters Shop. 62: plate, Inshop. 64: marble, W. E. Grant & Co. (Marble) Ltd. 66: top: plate, Fortnum & Mason. 67: plates, Villeroy & Boch. 68: plates, Villeroy & Boch; fork, Mappin & Webb Silversmiths; marble, W. E. Grant & Co. (Marble)

Ltd. 69: plate, Royal Worcester, Worcester; marble, W. E. Grant & Co. (Marble) Ltd. 70: plate, Hutschenreuther (U.K.) Ltd.; fork, Mappin & Webb Silversmiths. 71: china, The Conran Shop. 73: china, Villeroy & Boch. 75: plate, The Conran Shop. 76: china, Villeroy & Boch. 77: china, Hutschenreuther (U.K.) Ltd.; silver, Mappin & Webb Silversmiths. 78: plate, Chinacraft Ltd.; marble, W. E. Grant & Co. (Marble) Ltd. 79: china, Chinacraft Ltd.; fork, Mappin & Webb Silversmiths; cake stand, Line of Scandinavia. 81: china, Hutschenreuther (U.K.) Ltd.; napkin, Kilkenny. 82: large plate, Rosenthal (London) Ltd. 84: china, Royal Worcester, Worcester; lace cloth, Laura Ashley Ltd. 85: plate, Spode, Worcester. 86: china, Hutschenreuther (U.K.) Ltd.; fork, Mappin & Webb Silversmiths; cloth, Ewart Liddell. 88: fork, Mappin & Webb Silversmiths. 89, 90: marble, W. E. Grant & Co. (Marble) Ltd. 91: plate, Hutschenreuther (U.K.) Ltd.; fork, Mappin & Webb Silversmiths. 94: plates, Inshop. 95: china, Hutschenreuther (U.K.) Ltd.; marble, W. E. Grant & Co. (Marble) Ltd. 98: china, Royal Worcester, Worcester. 100: marble, W. E. Grant & Co. (Marble) Ltd. 101: china, Hutschenreuther (U.K.) Ltd. 102, 103, 109, 112: marble, W. E. Grant & Co. (Marble) Ltd. 115: lace cloth, Laura Ashley Ltd. 116: plates, Rosenthal (London) Ltd. 117: platter, Fortnum & Mason; plate, Royal Worcester, Worcester. 118: china, Hutschenreuther (U.K.) Ltd. 120: plate, Royal Worcester, Worcester; marble, W. E. Grant & Co. (Marble) Ltd. 122: marble, W. E. Grant & Co. (Marble) Ltd. 124: china, Hutschenreuther (U.K.) Ltd. 125, 127: marble, W. E. Grant & Co. (Marble) Ltd. 128: top plate, Hutschenreuther (U.K.) Ltd.; marble, W. E. Grant & Co. (Marble) Ltd. 130: plate, Hutschenreuther (U.K.) Ltd. 131: platter, Royal Worcester, Worcester; marble, W. E. Grant & Co. (Marble) Ltd. 132: plate, Hutschenreuther (U.K.) Ltd.; tablecloth, Ewart Liddell. 135: candlestick, Mappin & Webb Silversmiths. 136: marble, W. E. Grant & Co. (Marble) Ltd. 137: china, Hutschenreuther (U.K.) Ltd.

Acknowledgments

The editors also with to thank the following: Paul van Biene, London; René Bloom, London; Maureen Burrows, London; Alexandra Carlier, London; Windsor Chorlton, London; Eleanor Coleman, London; Jonathan Driver, London; Neil Fairbairn, Wivenhoe, Essex; Formica, Newcastle, Tyne and Wear; Tim Fraser, London; Irena Hoare, London; Molly Hodgson, Richmond, Yorkshire; Perstorp Warerite Ltd., London; Mario Pezzotta, London; Katherine Reeve, London; Sharp Electronics (U.K.) Ltd., London; Jane Stevenson, London; Miranda Tonbridge, London; Toshiba (U.K.) Ltd., London.

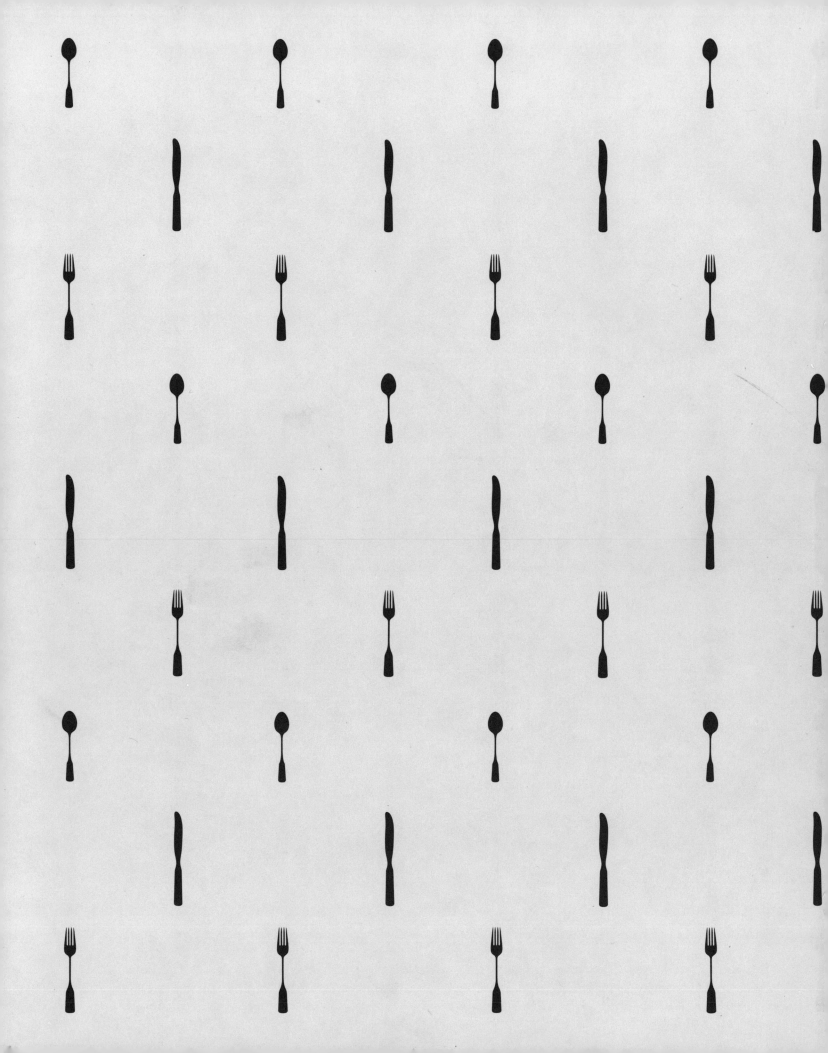